POLICE WRITING

POLICE WRITING:
A Guide to the Essentials

KELLY ROGERS RUPP
Redlands Community College
El Reno, Oklahoma

PEARSON
Prentice
Hall

Upper Saddle River, New Jersey 07458

Library of Congress Cataloging-in-Publication Data

Rogers Rupp, Kelly.
  Police writing : a guide to the essentials / Kelly Rogers Rupp.
      p. cm.
Includes index.
  ISBN 0-13-098189-3 (pbk. : alk. paper)
  1. Police—Authorship 2. Police reports. 3. Report writing. 4. Criminal investigation. I. Title.

HV7936.R53R52 2004
808'.066363—dc22

2003025967

Executive Editor: Frank Mortimer
Editor-in-Chief: Stephen Helba
Assistant Editor: Sarah Holle
Managing Editor: Mary Carnis
Production Liaison: Brian Hyland
Manufacturing Buyer: Cathleen Petersen
Director of Manufacturing and Production:
  Bruce Johnson

Design Director: Cheryl Asherman
Senior Design Coordinator: Miguel Ortiz
Cover Designer: Carey Davies
Cover Image: Paul A. Sorders/CORBIS
Composition/Full-Service Project Management:
  Laserwords/nSight
Printer/Binder: Phoenix–Book Tech

Notice: The author and the publisher of this volume have taken care to make certain that the information given is correct and compatible with the standards generally accepted at the time of publication. Nevertheless, as new information becomes available, changes in treatment and in the use of equipment and procedures become necessary. The reader is advised to carefully consult the instructions and information material included in each piece of equipment or device before administration. Students are warned that the use of any techniques must be authorized by their medical adviser, where appropriate, in accord with local laws and regulations. The author and publisher disclaim any liability, loss, injury, or damage incurred as a consequence, directly or indirectly, of the use and application of any of the contents of this book.

Pearson Education LTD.
Pearson Education Singapore, Pte. Ltd
Pearson Education, Canada, Ltd
Pearson Education—Japan

Pearson Education Australia PTY, Limited
Pearson Education North Asia Ltd
Pearson Educación de Mexico, S.A. de C.V.
Pearson Education Malaysia, Pte. Ltd

10 9 8 7 6 5 4 3 2 1
ISBN 0-13-098189-3

To Gabe, Zach, and Allie

CONTENTS

———— • ◆ • ————

CHAPTER 7   RESEARCHING

CHAPTER 8   ORGANIZING AND DRAFTING

CHAPTER 9   DOCUMENTATION STYLE

Contents

CHAPTER 10   A BRIEF HANDBOOK OF ENGLISH   *164*

COMMON ERRORS IN SENTENCE MECHANICS   165

Sentence Fragments: The Dead End Streets of English 165

Comma Splices and Run-Ons: Running the Stop Signs 171

COMMON ERRORS IN GRAMMAR   175

Subject–Verb Agreement 175

Pronoun Problems 176

Dangling Modifiers 177

Misplaced Modifiers 177

Wordiness 178

PUNCTUATION   178

End Punctuation 178

Commas 178

COMMONLY MISSPELLED WORDS   *181*

INDEX   *185*

Preface

———————•◆•———————

This book is a short, student- and instructor-friendly guide to writing for law enforcement students and practitioners. It is intended for use as the primary text for a writing for law enforcement class, a supplemental text for introductory-level law enforcement and criminal justice classes, a training manual for police academies, and a resource manual for police departments and practitioners.

In the process of preparing materials for the Council on Law Enforcement Education and Training (CLEET) and continuing education training for law enforcement professionals, I have visited with law enforcement instructors and administrators who are concerned about the writing skills of police officers.

As I reviewed professional samples of good and not-so-good writing, it struck me that what these writers need is a set of guidelines and good models for writing. With that goal in mind, I have relied on police chiefs to provide samples of reports and other writing projects that they consider to be good. Who better to provide the models than the people who are returning reports and asking for revisions? I have also spent many hours talking to police chiefs to determine what elements they look for in a good report.

With their responses in mind, I met with law enforcement instructors to find out what challenges they feel their students have in writing for academic work. Many of these instructors assign research papers, but they don't have time to teach the course content as well as to teach students how to write the required papers. Students taking introductory-level classes may not have completed English I, and some degree programs do not require English II, so these students sometimes have no idea how to approach writing a research paper.

After meeting with both groups, it seemed clear that my text needed to include academic and professional writing sections.

The academic writing portion of this text is a guide to writing a research paper, from coming up with an idea to producing the final draft. I have also included brief guides for Modern Language Association (MLA), American Psychological Association (APA), and American Sociological Association (ASA) style and a brief handbook of English.

The professional portion of the text is dedicated to actual writing tasks that officers will be asked to complete on the job. I have placed emphasis on writing the narrative portion of the report. Additionally, during my discussions with police chiefs and officers, a topic that came up repeatedly was the need for more funding for police departments. To address this, I have included a section on grant writing.

Features of this text include:

- An overview of writing styles and tasks
- Guidelines and models for professional writing tasks
- Guidelines for writing grant proposals
- Guidelines and models for writing letters and memos
- Guidelines and models for writing cover letters and resumes
- A step-by-step approach to writing a research paper
- A brief handbook of English
- Chapter activities

It is my intent that this text will serve as a valuable teaching tool for criminal justice instructors, specifically at the community college level. Additionally, I hope that practitioners will use this book in the workplace to help them with the multitude of writing tasks they will encounter.

TO THE STUDENT

So you chose to become a cop because you love to write, right? Okay, probably not. Like it or not, though, as an officer, you will create loads of paperwork and lots of different people will be reading that paperwork.

The purpose of this book is to help you become comfortable with the writing tasks you will need to do at work as well as at school.

Students are often intimidated by writing; they view themselves as poor writers and view writing as a dreaded task. But it doesn't have to be hard!

This book is divided into three sections:

- Writing for a Purpose
- Writing for Law Enforcement
- Writing for Academia

Writing for a Purpose is designed to teach you to analyze the writing task to determine its purpose and audience. This unit explores different types of writing tasks and which types of writing are appropriate to those tasks. The unit explores different writing styles as well as the elements of good writing.

Writing for Law Enforcement offers students specific guidelines and examples of on-the-job writing. In addition to covering incident reports, accident reports, search warrant affidavits and returns, and arrest warrant affidavits and returns, this unit offers instruction in writing letters and memos, grant proposals, short reports, and resumes.

Writing for Academia walks you through the process of writing a research paper, from planning the paper through preparing the final draft. Three different documentation styles are outlined, and a brief review of English is included.

This book should be a keeper. The idea behind the content is that you can use the book while you are in college to complete your class-related writing tasks as well as after you graduate and begin your career. The materials concerning on-the-job writing tasks are provided so that you can refer back to this book for help when you have to write during your job, be it report narratives or grants.

TO THE INSTRUCTOR

Writing across the curriculum has become an essential on college campuses. In fact, most introductory-level content classes require some sort of research paper. And law enforcement administrators expect incoming officers to have a command of written language and proficiency in job-related writing tasks.

So where does this leave you? You need to devote your time to teaching the content of your courses, not to teaching writing. This book is designed to take the burden of teaching writing off of you.

Many criminal justice and law enforcement departments are creating specialized writing courses for their students. This book is designed to serve as a primary text for such a course. The chances of an instructor being both a writing specialist and a law enforcement practitioner are slim, so this text is explanatory enough that a specialist in either area can teach the content.

In an attempt to make your job easier, I have included sections on both professional and academic writing. With this book you can customize your writing assignments to meet the needs of your students and your curriculum.

The professional writing section of this text includes guidelines and models for:

- Incident reports
- Non-fatality vehicle accidents
- Fatality vehicle accidents

- Search warrant affidavits
- Search warrants
- Search warrant returns
- Arrest warrant affidavits
- Arrest warrants
- Arrest warrant returns
- Grant proposals
- Letters and memos
- Short reports

The academic writing section of the book includes the following instructions for writing a research paper:

- Defining the assignment
- Brainstorming ideas
- Conducting research
- Organizing information
- Writing the first draft
- Revising and editing
- Documenting sources
- Citing references
- Formatting the manuscript

Other features of this text include a brief handbook of English, chapter summaries, and suggested activities.

Whether you are using this book as a primary text or as a course supplement, it has been written to include everything you need to make helping your students with the writing tasks they will need at work and at school as easy as possible.

Acknowledgments

—◆—

I would like to thank:

Jerry Boyer, Delores Meyer, and Bruce Storm for their encouragement and knowledge.

Lt. Ken Brown and Chief Ed Smith for their expertise and relevant sample reports.

Jackie Weekly for keeping the contracts coming and Ruby Guthrie for tech support.

In addition, I would like to thank the following people, who reviewed the manuscript and offered helpful suggestions and comments: Suzann W. Barr (University of Arkansas), Alex del Carmen (University of Texas–Arlington), Ellen Cohen (Florida International University), David R. Kotajarvi (Lakeshore Technical College), and Jody Sundt (Southern Illinois University).

UNIT I

Writing for a Purpose

1 *Report Writing Style*

A. WHAT IS STYLE?
   1. Writing Style
   2. Documentation Style
B. THE SEVEN C'S OF CRIMINAL JUSTICE WRITING
   1. Complete
   2. Concise
   3. Clear
   4. Concrete
   5. Correct
   6. Considerate and Courteous
C. SUMMARY
D. ACTIVITIES

WHAT IS STYLE?

In writing, style refers to the way you write your paper. This includes subject, tone, sentence length, paragraph development, word choice, graphics, and documentation style. The style that you are probably familiar with is the style you learned in English Composition I and II: expository writing using Modern Language Association (MLA) style. In fact, you probably had a manual like this for MLA style, or it might have been a section of your English book.

Writing Style

In your English Composition I and II classes, you probably used expository style. That means you used colorful language, long sentences, long paragraphs, and vivid descriptions. Your instructor probably told you to provide sufficient support by adding examples, definitions, and descriptions. Your instructors in composition classes asked you to interpret and analyze essays and issues. They asked you to form an opinion and then defend it.

In terms of style, criminal justice writing is very different from expository writing. In fact, in many ways, it is exactly the opposite. The K.I.S.S. method (Keep It Short and Simple) is a rule of thumb for criminal justice writing. You may have to write a 10-page research paper, but it needs to be full of facts, figures, observations, and direct quotes rather than interpretation, personal feelings, and speculation. Your writing for criminal justice will more closely resemble newspaper style than expository style (see Box 1.1).

Documentation Style

Documentation style refers to the way that you give credit to your sources. When you write a research paper you gather facts and ideas from a number of sources.

Box 1.1.   Expository style vs. technical style

Expository Style (English Composition)	Technical Style (Criminal Justice)	Journalistic Style (Newspapers)
Long sentences	Short sentences	Short sentences
Interpretation	Observation	Observation
Third person	First person	Third person
Subjective	Objective	Objective
Graphics prohibited	Graphics encouraged	Graphics encouraged
MLA style	JQ or APA style	AP style

Any time that you include an idea that you have borrowed from someone else you must **document** that source. If you don't, you will have committed **plagiarism**, which is the act of presenting someone else's ideas as your own. Most colleges have strict penalties for plagiarism. You must attribute quotations (word for word ideas) and paraphrases (someone else's ideas put into your own words) used in your paper by adding parenthetical notation, footnotes, or endnotes. You must also provide a bibliography, which is a list of the complete bibliographic notation (author, title, publisher, date, page numbers), for each of the references you have used.

Documentation style tells you how to attribute your sources. It may seem picky, but every bit of information must be included exactly as your style specifies—that includes commas, colons, and periods in exactly the right places. Instructions for documentation are included in Chapter 9. Right now we'll concentrate on the writing style used in criminal justice.

THE SEVEN C'S OF CRIMINAL JUSTICE WRITING

As you read earlier, criminal justice writing more closely resembles journalistic writing (the kind you read in the newspapers) than expository writing. The purpose of writing is to communicate information to the reader. News reporters and police officers both gather information through researching existing documentation, interviewing relevant sources, such as witnesses and experts, and recording personal observations. This information is gathered as it becomes available and recorded in field notes.

Although the writing tasks may appear to be different, they are amazingly similar. Both a police officer and a news reporter must organize the information they have gathered into a coherent recounting of the events. Reporters use an inverted pyramid style to write a story. That means they answer the most important questions first and then follow with more minor details. Police officers tend to use a chronological—time order—approach in writing a narrative report.

With these elements in mind, the criminal justice writer must follow the seven C's of writing:

- Complete
- Concise
- Clear
- Concrete
- Correct
- Considerate
- Courteous

A report answers all of the relevant questions. This applies to any writing you might do, from a research paper to a crime report. As a writer of information, you must decide what information is relevant to your writing task and then seek answers to those questions through primary or secondary research. Primary research is taken from you firsthand through direct observations or from personal interviews with experts or witnesses. Secondary research is taken from written sources such as other reports, databases, or articles.

Complete

A report must answer all of the relevant questions for the task. A research paper will require different types of information than an incident report, and it is the writer's task to determine what information must be included and what information is unnecessary. No matter what the task, the questions of who, what, when, where, why, and how must be answered as completely as possible.

Imagine that you are writing a research paper about how the Miranda vs. Arizona case affects police officers. You would need to answer the following questions and then decide which answers are relevant to the research paper.

Selection 1: Miranda vs. Arizona*

Ernesto Miranda was arrested at his home in Phoenix, Arizona, and taken into custody at a Phoenix police station on March 13, 1963. A witness identified him at the police station. Miranda was taken to an interrogation room and questioned by police for two hours. The officers emerged with a written confession signed by Miranda, prefaced with a typed paragraph stating that the confession was made voluntarily, without pressure and with "full knowledge of my legal rights, understanding any statement I make may be used against me."

The written confession was entered into evidence at the jury trial over the defense counsel's objection, and the police officers testified to Miranda's oral confession during interrogation. Miranda was convicted of kidnapping and rape and was sentenced to 20 to 30 years' concurrent imprisonment on each count. The Supreme Court of Arizona upheld the conviction, emphasizing that Miranda did not request counsel. Miranda appealed to the U.S. Supreme Court.

The United States Supreme Court reversed the ruling on the following merits:

1. By admission of the police officers who obtained the statement, Miranda was not advised of his right to consult with legal counsel and have legal counsel present during questioning.
2. Miranda was not advised of his right to avoid self incrimination.
3. Without being informed of his legal rights before making his statements, Miranda's statements were not admissible as evidence.

*Printed courtesy of Lawinfo.com.

4. The typed preface on the written confession did not fulfill the requirement for a knowing and intelligent waiver, which is required to relinquish constitutional rights.

5. The Fifth Amendment privilege against self-incrimination and the Sixth Amendment right to counsel are not mutually exclusive rights. They may overlap in some instances and protect the interests of the accused in an interrogation setting.

6. Without being told he had the right to remain silent, that anything he said could be used against him in a court of law, that he had the right to an attorney, and that if he could not afford one the court would appoint a lawyer, Miranda could not knowingly waive his rights.

7. Miranda was deprived of both his Fifth Amendment right to avoid self incrimination and his Sixth Amendment right to counsel.

Questions for Miranda vs. Arizona

Who Questions
Who was Miranda?
Who arrested and questioned him?
Who else was involved?
Who sentenced him?
Who reversed the decision?
Who wrote the decision?
Who is affected by the decision?

What Questions
What happened?
What was the Arizona verdict?
What was Miranda's sentence?
What was the Supreme Court ruling?
What were the grounds for that ruling?
What were the effects of the ruling?

When Questions
When was Miranda arrested?
When did the Supreme Court render its decision?
When was the Miranda ruling overturned?
When must suspects be informed of their rights?
When is it unnecessary to inform a suspect of his/her rights?

Where Questions
Where was Miranda arrested?
Where was the initial ruling rendered?
Where was the ruling overturned?
Where are Miranda rights used?

Why Questions
Why did the Supreme Court overturn the Arizona ruling?
Why should officers be aware of the Miranda case?
Why do suspects need to be informed of their rights?
Why is this a precedent-setting case?

How Questions
How should officers act on the Miranda ruling?
How has Miranda changed interrogation practices?
How can the Miranda decision affect a case?

Next, imagine that you are preparing to write the narrative report for the burglary in Selection 2. You need to answer the relevant questions in the report and discard the information that is not necessary.

Selection 2: Burglary Investigation

You have been called to the scene of a burglary. The call is dispatched to you at 5:45 p.m. on May 12, 1999. The address was 412 Robin's Nest Circle, Pittsburg, Kansas. The doorknob on the garage door is on the floor in the utility room. The owners of the home are Robert Lee Vaughn and Vera Sue Vaughn. Also residing in the home are Lisa Marie Vaughn and Richard Lloyd Vaughn, the daughter and son of the homeowners. You observe no other signs of entry. Mr. Vaughn escorts you to Lisa Marie's room. You observe a black substance on the walls spelling out the words "I'll get you, bitch." The substance is still wet. You also observe a can of black spray paint on the floor beside Lisa Marie's bed. The items Lisa Marie reports missing are an estimated 75 compact discs of music, an AWAI portable compact disc player, and her diary. Lisa Marie tells you that she last saw these items right before the entire family left the house together at 7:45 a.m. that day. No one in the family had been to the house during the day until they all returned home to discover the break-in. Richard Vaughn's date of birth is February 3, 1983, and his social security number is 000-01-0001; Lisa Marie Vaughn's date of birth is December 1, 1985, and her social security number is 000-05-5000; Robert Vaughn's date of birth is March 4, 1960, and his social security number is 000-06-0600; Vera Vaughn's date of birth is June 25, 1960, and her social security number is 000-08-0811. Robert Vaughn is an architect employed with Vaughn, Vaughn, and Vaughn at 333 Main Street, Pittsburg, Kansas. His work phone is 316-555-5555. Vera Vaughn is a physical therapist at Parkview Hospital in Pittsburg, Kansas. Her work phone is 316-555-0000. Robert Vaughn tells you that he discovered the break-in when the family arrived home together at 5:40. Mr. Vaughn mentions that Lisa Marie has just broken up with her boyfriend and that he has been making threatening phone calls for the past four days. The boyfriend's name is Billy Simms. His address is 325 Mockingbird Road, Pittsburg, Kansas. You leave the scene after checking all of the doors and windows for additional possible entry and finding nothing disturbed. You leave the residence at 6:15 p.m.

Questions for the Burglary Investigation Narrative

Who Questions*
Who reported the crime?
Who discovered the crime?

Who else has knowledge of the crime?
Who responded to the call?
Who are potential witnesses?

Who are possible suspects?
*Note: Crime report "who" questions must include correctly spelled, complete names, dates of birth, social security numbers, home addresses, telephone numbers, and workplace names, addresses, and phone numbers.

What Questions

What happened?
What was reported missing?
What was the method of entry?
What was the modus operandi?
What are the possible motives?
What evidence is present?
What leads need to be followed up?

When Questions

When was the crime reported?
When did the officer arrive at the scene?
When was the crime discovered?
When could the crime have occurred?

When were the missing items last seen?
When did the officer leave the scene?
When will you follow up?

Where Questions

Where did the crime take place?
Where were the residents at the time of the crime?
Where was the suspect?
Where were the missing items last seen?
Where was the evidence found?

Why Questions

Why was this location targeted?
Why were these items taken?

How Questions

How was the crime discovered?
How did the perpetrator gain entry?
How did the perpetrator exit the crime scene?
How many items are missing?
How much are the missing items worth?
How is this crime scene similar to other crime scenes?

As you begin answering the critical questions, you will probably find that you need additional information. Make a list of the information you need and do more research. For a research paper, this means you need to locate reference materials from secondary sources such as magazines, newspapers, books, and the Internet. If you are writing a narrative report about an incident, you may need to question witnesses and suspects further.

Remember that a well-written report is complete because it answers all of the relevant questions.

Concise

Writing concisely means keeping your writing exact. Have you ever had a friend tell you a long and winding story? When someone recounts an event, he or she often goes off into related tangents as they occur to him or her. This can be extremely confusing. Writers face the same problem. Just because you know what you mean does not necessarily mean your reader can follow your line of logic.

In order to write concisely, you must omit wordy expressions, include only relevant statements, and avoid unnecessary repetition. These are obstacles to clear communication.

Omit Wordiness

To omit wordiness, keep the K.I.S.S. method in mind. There is no need to "dress up" your writing by padding it with unnecessary words. Box 1.2 provides a list of common wordy phrases and some more concise options.

Include Only Relevant Information

Another stumbling block to good communication occurs when writers include information that is not necessary. Wading through unnecessary information can tire the reader and lead to his or her missing critical information buried within extraneous details.

After you answer the kinds of critical questions listed earlier in this chapter, you must decide which answers need to be included in your report. If you were writing a research paper about the Miranda case, would it be necessary to include how many officers were employed by the Phoenix police department or what kind of cruisers they drove? Of course not! These bits of information have no bearing on the Miranda case. Although the answer to this question is obvious, there will be times when you will have to make judgment calls.

Box 1.2. Eliminating wordy phrases

Wordy	Better	Wordy	Better
Due to the fact that	Because	At the present time	Now
In the event that	If	To begin with	First
In the near future	Soon	Active consideration	Consideration
Until such time as	Until	As a matter of fact	In fact
At all times	Always	In order to	To
During the time that	When	With regard to	About
Make assumptions about	Assume	Came to the conclusion	Concluded
Along the lines of	Like	In spite of the fact	Despite
An additional	Another	For the purpose of	For

Box 1.3.   Search engine matches to "Miranda vs. Arizona"

Search Engine	Lycos	Yahoo	Hotbot	Excite	Infoseek
Number of Matches	140	423	666	745,680	3,598,911

Internet searches provide an excellent example of the need to evaluate the relevance of information. Consider Box 1.3, which shows the number of matches (hits) to "Miranda vs. Arizona" using some common search engines.

Obviously, you won't be able to read every Web site that comes up as a match in your search, but you can read the site descriptions and narrow the list to the sites that seem related to your topic.

Creating an outline can help you to weed out the unnecessary information. A good practice to follow in deciding what information to include is to constantly ask, "What does this have to do with what I am trying to communicate?" If the answer isn't obvious, the information can probably be excluded.

Box 1.4.   Eliminating repetition

Repetitive	Concise	Repetitive	Concise
Hollow tube	Tube	Completely eliminated	Eliminated
Circle around	Circle	Close proximity	Proximity
Cooperate together	Cooperate	Completely unanimous	Unanimous
Final completion	Completion	Completely eliminate	Eliminate
Absolutely essential	Essential	Exactly identical	Identical
Fair and equitable	Equitable	True facts	Facts
New innovations	Innovations	Repeat again	Repeat
Final solution	Solution	Final conclusion	Conclusion
Completely surrounded	Surrounded	Brief summary	Summary
Total absence	Absence	Past history	Past
Each and every	Each	End result	Result

Avoid Repetition

Many writers think that more is better when it comes to words. This is not the case. There are many commonly used phrases that are repetitive. For example, has anyone ever told you that she woke up at 6:00 a.m. in the morning? Certainly it isn't necessary to use both phrases because "a.m." means "in the morning". Use Box 1.4 as a guide for eliminating these redundant phrases from your writing.

Readers rarely have an opportunity to complete a reading task undisturbed. How many times are you interrupted by a telephone call, a knock at the door, or a need to get up to get something? You can make a reader's job easier by keeping your language concise.

Compare the two memos in Figure 1.1 and Figure 1.2 to see which is easier to read.

Interoffice Memo

Date: 3/15/04
To: Chief Smiley
From: Officer Dudley Doright
RE: Escape of Snidely Whiplash

I am writing in accordance with your request in reference to the events that led up to the escape of Snidely Whiplash from my custody. In the event that I recapture Mr. Whiplash, I shall endeavor to assure that Mr. Whiplash does not have occasion to escape from my custody again.

To begin with, I had detained Mr. Whiplash and had him tied across my horse, which I was riding. At that time, I heard screams coming from the railroad tracks. Upon changing my course and approaching the railroad tracks for the reason that I had heard screams, I ascertained that Nell, a local townswoman, had at a previous time been tethered to the tracks. During the time that I was coming to the conclusion that she needed to be untied, I realized that a train was coming towards her faster than a speeding bullet. I got off of my horse for the reason of freeing Nell. Irregardless of the danger to myself, I approached the railroad tracks by leaps and bounds.

At the time that I was untying Nell from her bondage, needless to say, I was concentrating on the task in front of me. Nell's mother was a cousin by marriage to my great aunt. At that point in time Mr. Whiplash took advantage of my obvious preoccupation with the situation at hand and managed to get away slippery as an eel.

Please be advised that I will be seeking to apprehend Mr. Whiplash in due course.

Figure 1.1.   Wordy Memorandum

Interoffice Memo

Date: 3/15/04
To: Chief Smiley
From: Officer Dudley Doright
RE: Escape of Snidely Whiplash

I am writing to explain how Snidely Whiplash escaped from my custody. When I recapture Mr. Whiplash, I will not allow him to escape again.

On March 12, 2004, I had Mr. Whiplash restrained and in my custody when I heard screams coming from the railroad tracks. When I reached the tracks, I saw Nell, a local townswoman, tied to the tracks. I saw a train was coming, so I got off of my horse to untie Nell.

While I was preoccupied, Mr. Whiplash escaped.

I will try to recapture Mr. Whiplash tomorrow.

Figure 1.2. Concise Memorandum

The key to concise writing is editing; never assume that a first draft is ready to be submitted. Wordy phrases, irrelevant information, and repetitive language should be edited to eliminate these pitfalls to concise writing.

Clear

Clarity is also essential for effective writing. Writing clearly means using understandable language, complete sentences, developed paragraphs, and, when appropriate, graphics, such as tables and illustrations.

Use Understandable Language

A thesaurus is a wonderful tool for student writers, but you have to be careful not to obscure your meaning by using words that are too complicated. Can you figure out what common sayings are being rephrased in the following selections?

A unit of monetary exchange conserved is a unit of monetary exchange merited.

At no time bemoan overturned liquid dairy products.

It is preferable to have experienced deep emotional feelings of affection and been defeated in the pursuit of the object of this emotion than to have deprived oneself of ever having experienced these emotional characteristics.

Writers often try to impress readers by using long words and complicated language. The key to deciding what is appropriate is determining the sophistication of your audience. You should adjust your language to fit your audience all the time. For example, you would not use the same language with your grandmother that you use with your friends; you unconsciously adapt your language to fit the situation. In most cases, you should use simple language to get your message across.

Write Complete Sentences

The first rule of good writing is to write complete sentences. A complete sentence contains a subject and a verb and expresses a complete thought. A fragment is a sentence that is missing a subject or a complete verb or does not express a complete thought.

Missing Subject Fragments

Was followed closely by the car.
I was followed closely by the car.
Refused treatment in spite of her injuries.
Mrs. Smith refused treatment in spite of her injuries.

Missing Verb Fragments

The suspect walking through the park in a suspicious manner.
The suspect **was walking** through the park in a suspicious manner.
Mr. Jones driving the wrong way down a one-way street.
Mr. Jones **was driving** the wrong way down a one-way street.

Incomplete Thought Fragments

While I was driving down the street.
While I was driving down the street, **I observed the suspect**.
Until I came to a complete stop.
I did not get out of the car, Until I came to a compete stop.

For more information about writing complete sentences, refer to Chapter 10.

Develop Paragraphs

Development is critical in any writing task. You must support what you are saying with specific details. Each paragraph must have a topic sentence, supporting details, and a concluding sentence. In technical writing tasks, a paragraph should be about five to seven sentences long.

A topic sentence tells the reader what the paragraph is about without making an announcement such as: "This paragraph will explain how to document an incident." Instead, you might write, "Officers should avoid wordy expressions when documenting an incident report." The reader now knows what you are going to discuss and that further explanation and specific examples will follow.

Supporting details would include examples of wordy expressions. A paragraph that explains how to avoid wordy expressions might define wordy expressions and offer specific examples. It is important to offer adequate and specific support for a paragraph. It is also important to make sure that all of the supporting evidence is relevant to the paragraph.

When you begin an area of discussion not relevant to your paragraph's topic sentence, it's time to start a new paragraph. It is good writing practice to end a paragraph with a bridging sentence—one that guides the reader into the next paragraph smoothly.

Include Graphics

Graphics are extremely helpful to a reader when numbers are being compared or when a concept needs to be visualized. They also break up black and white text and draw the reader's attention. Always label tables, illustrations, and figures, and clearly refer to them in the body of your paper.

Concrete

Concrete writing uses exact facts and figures. Concrete writing also uses action verbs and avoids vague terms. Stay away from passive verbs such as "have been spoken," and "have been observed." Instead use the active verbs—"spoke" and "observed." You should also avoid vague terms like "a little," "a lot," "close," and "far away." Instead, you should use more specific terms, such as "a quarter of a gram," "three hundred pounds," "six inches," and "five miles."

Correct

Correct writing leaves no room for guesswork. Always use correct statistical figures, spellings of names, street addresses, and supporting information. Always double-check the accuracy of the numbers you use in writing. Pay special attention to this!

There are no small mistakes in police report writing. A misspelled name can lead to the wrong person being named as a suspect; an incorrectly recorded time can result in dropped charges; one wrong number in an address can result in officers serving a warrant to the wrong house. These things can and do happen, sometimes resulting in lawsuits and departmental embarrassment.

Using standard English is another element of correct writing. Follow the rules of style and grammar and proofread carefully to ensure that your writing is correct.

Considerate and Courteous

A considerate and courteous writer never interjects inappropriate material into a writing project. Unsupported speculation, racist or sexist language, or offensive language (unless it is in a quotation) has no place in a written report. This will be especially important when you begin writing narrative reports that can be entered into evidence in court. Off-color remarks may seem funny to you and to your peers, but defense attorneys can use them to bring your character into question. Remember Mark Fuhrman from the O.J. Simpson trial?

As a law enforcement professional, you must be objective in your writing. That means you don't interject your personal opinions unless they are requested. You must also apply ethics and professionalism to your writing. This includes your field notes, which can be subpoenaed by the court. Do not write offensive comments of any kind in your field notes or reports unless you are directly quoting someone you've interviewed or comments you've overheard.

Consider the following bumper sticker:

Bad Cop
No Donut

While amusing to some people, this bumper sticker reinforces stereotypes about police officers. How does that make you feel? Is the car sporting this bumper sticker more or less likely to be pulled over for a minor traffic violation? What is funny to one person might be highly offensive to another.

Another element of courteous writing is response time. Always respond to writing requests promptly. In college, this means turning in your papers on time. Late papers can carry grade penalties. But there is a larger issue at stake here. College deadlines are designed to get you into the habit of submitting work on time. Employees who habitually miss deadlines can be denied promotion or be marked down on evaluation. Cases may be dismissed if paperwork is not completed, and this can allow guilty parties to go free on technicalities. Always turn reports in on time.

Who was Mark Fuhrman?

Mark Fuhrman was a detective in the Los Angeles Police Department. He was among the first to arrive at the Nicole Simpson/Ron Goldman crime scene, and he accompanied two senior LAPD detectives to the O.J. Simpson residence. Fuhrman was the detective who found the bloody glove.

During the Simpson trial, Fuhrman was called as a witness for the prosecution. In cross examination the defense questioned Fuhrman about alleged racial remarks that he had made over the course of his career. Under oath, Fuhrman denied ever having used racial epithets, specifically the N-word.

The defense then produced a witness who testified that taped statements existed in which Fuhrman could be heard using racial epithets. Additionally, the defense produced three more witnesses who testified about Fuhrman's use of racial epithets.

Having discredited Fuhrman as a witness, the defense later called him to the stand as a witness for the defense, where he invoked his Fifth Amendment right not to incriminate himself.

Fuhrman was later charged with and convicted of perjury. On a larger scale, though, the discrediting of this key witness—and, by extension, the bloody glove that he claimed to have found—weakened the entire case and, ultimately, cost Fuhrman his career in law enforcement.

SUMMARY

In writing, style refers to the way you write and document your sources in a particular field of study. Criminal justice writing uses a tight style that is much closer to journalistic writing than to expository writing.

The purpose of criminal justice writing is to convey the necessary information as clearly and concisely as possible. Short words, short sentences, and short paragraphs are the preferred style for criminal justice writing.

A criminal justice writer is careful to be:

Complete

　　Answers all relevant questions

Concise

　　Omits wordiness
　　Includes only relevant information
　　Avoids unnecessary repetition

Clear

    Uses understandable language

    Uses complete sentences

    Develops paragraphs

Concrete

    Incorporates facts and figures

    Chooses active verbs

    Avoids vague words

Correct

    Uses appropriate language for the audience

    Includes only accurate facts

    Uses correct English

Considerate and Courteous

    Maintains objectivity

    Omits profanity (unless necessary and quoted)

    Applies integrity and ethics

    Omits racist and sexist language

    Submits reports on time

ACTIVITIES

1. List and define the elements of good writing as discussed in this chapter.
2. Create your own list of wordy expressions. Give your list to a classmate and have the classmate find more concise terms.
3. Rewrite a famous saying in wordy terms. Exchange your wordy version with a classmate and have the classmate find the original saying.
4. Using the information provided in *Selection 2: Burglary Investigation*, write a narrative incorporating the elements of a good report.
5. Write a memo explaining why you missed class on a particular day. Incorporate the concepts addressed in this chapter.

2

Planning and Organizing

WHY ARE PLANNING AND ORGANIZING IMPORTANT?

Many people believe that a mystique surrounds the art of writing. They have a pre-conceived picture of a writer sitting down at the computer (or, more romantically, taking pen in hand) and waiting for inspiration to strike. They envision that when the magical moment comes, a choir sings as a single sunbeam lights up the newly inspired author, who promptly begins a frenzied writing spree.

These people are both right and wrong. There truly is a waiting period before the writing begins, but that time is actually spent planning the writing project, not waiting for inspiration.

The writing process can be broken down into three distinct stages:

- Prewriting
- Writing
- Revising

Each stage is critical to the process. As you become a more practiced writer, some of these stages may become more internal and automatic, but until you form good writing habits, make sure to carefully go through each stage.

PREWRITING

Prewriting serves as the first planning stage of writing. This step, which takes place before you begin writing, involves brainstorming and gathering prelimi-nary information. For example, if you were writing the narrative portion of a criminal investigation report, you would review your field notes and organize them into a chronological narrative account of the events. The prewriting por-tion of the narrative preparation would involve reviewing your field notes to re-fresh your memory and then making an outline of the timeline for each of the events.

In academic writing, your prewriting will usually be devoted to finding a topic that you want to write about and that meets the requirements of the writing assignment. Some instructors will give open writing assignments, leaving the topic up to the students, with some guidelines, such as keeping the topic related to something that has been covered in the course text or lectures or that is relevant to the content of the class. Other instructors will assign specific topics for the paper. In either case, it is up to you to determine what direction your paper will take and what area of the topic will be the primary focus. Prewriting is essential to this part of the writing task.

Choosing a Topic: Brainstorming Strategies

Brainstorming is the first step in prewriting. Brainstorming techniques are used to generate ideas for a writing project and to "get the juices flowing." Many writers approach a writing task expecting to create a final document at the first sitting, but this is an unrealistic expectation. How many times have you sat down to write and found yourself staring at an empty page thirty minutes later? Brainstorming strategies will help you to make better use of your writing time.

Here are three commonly used brainstorming techniques.

Free Writing

Free writing is a prewriting technique in which your primary goal is to just get some thoughts down on paper—there is no attention given to spelling, grammar, punctuation, transitional devices, or purpose. There are no rules for free writing (thus the "free" part of the phrase); the object is to get into a quiet place and write whatever comes into your mind, even if it doesn't seem to have anything to do with your writing task. Just let your mind wander, and eventually your writing will turn towards the project.

Another form of free writing is **focused free writing**, in which you give yourself a topic to inspire your free writing. For example, if your assignment is to write a paper about criminal investigation procedure, you might start out by jotting down everything you can remember about the topic. Focused free writing works best if you give yourself a set period of time and write continuously for that time.

Clustering

Clustering is another way for you to gather your thoughts. You start out with a circle in the middle of a blank page and then write the broad topic inside of the circle. From there, draw out lines and smaller circles with related ideas. Figure 2.1 shows an example of what clustering looks like.

Journaling

Journaling can be another form of brainstorming, but it requires time and patience. When you journal, you keep a log of information, feelings, reactions, and impressions to topics that are covered in class, items reported in the news, or to other information sources that you might find.

Keeping a journal of information that is relevant to a specific area of study can help you to come up with topics for your paper, but you have to be disciplined about making journal entries. You should make an entry at regular intervals—after class, for example—and keep to your schedule. If you keep good records of the topics, including writing a thorough discussion in each entry and recording each information source accurately, you can have a valuable research tool.

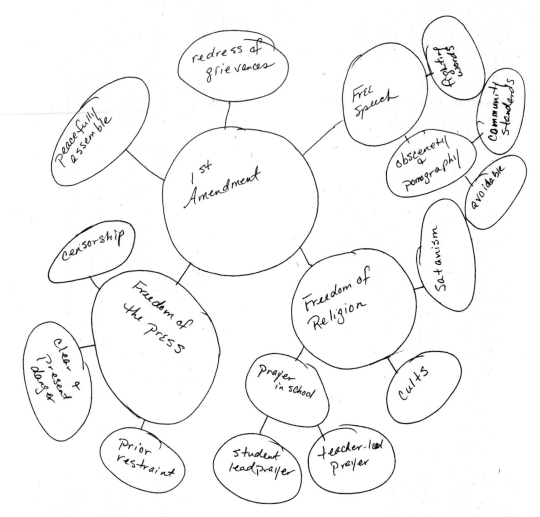

Figure 2.1.   Sample cluster

Expanding on Your Topic

After you have an idea of what you will write about, you will need to start gathering information from texts, newspapers, magazines, lectures, films, your notes, or any other place where you can find material about the topic.

Remember that you are still in the prewriting stage, so you can always drop some information later. For now, gather every piece of information related to your topic and start to make notes and/or lists of anything that might prove to be valuable when you begin writing. You can always add and drop things from your lists later as your writing product becomes clearer.

Make sure to make a notation of where you are getting your information so that, should you decide to use a particular fact or quotation, you can cite the source without having to dig through piles of reference material.

Determining Purpose

Any time you write, you must consider why you are writing (purpose) and to whom you are writing (audience). Determining your audience and purpose will help you to decide how to approach your writing task.

When determining your purpose, you must answer the following questions:

Why am I writing this document?

Student Applications

To reinforce and clarify class notes
To demonstrate mastery of course concepts
To demonstrate the ability to apply concepts
To convince the reader to take a
    recommended action
To submit to an instructor

Professional Applications

To clarify field notes
To give a narrative account of an incident
To provide a description of physical evidence
To convince the reader to take a recommended
    action
To submit to the investigating body
    (prosecuting attorney, lead detective)

What uses might this document have?

Student Applications

To serve as a test review
To fulfill a course requirement
To include in a student portfolio
To demonstrate writing competence

Professional Applications

To serve as a reminder
To present information for prosecution
To present information for defense
To present information for insurance investigators
To present information for the media

Answering these questions can help you analyze why you are writing a document. Having a purpose firmly set can assist you in staying on task throughout your writing project. Knowing why you are writing will help you to decide what information you want to include or drop from your initial research.

Determining Audience

After you have found a topic and determined your purpose, you need to identify your audience. This decision will be directly related to your writing purpose. Don't underestimate the importance of knowing the level of your reader because identifying your reader will determine what kind of language you will use.

If you are writing a paper for a class, the reader will probably be your professor, so you will need to adopt a formal tone. Although your professor knows about your topic, you will need to include detailed information because he or she will be reading the paper to ascertain your understanding of the concepts that you will be addressing. If the paper is for a criminal justice class, you can assume that jargon is acceptable; however, if you are writing about a criminal justice topic for an English composition class, then you will probably need to offer more explanations, as your instructor will probably have limited knowledge of this area.

In writing on the job, you will probably have multiple readers. For example, if you are writing a report about a crime investigation, you will be writing for readers both inside and outside of your agency. In this case, you might use your field notes to write a report, and then your report might become a part of a larger file. Depending on the case, your report might be read by detectives, prosecuting attorneys, defense attorneys, jurors, reporters, and judges. In this case, you must be aware of different levels of expertise.

WRITING

Once you have established your topic, audience, and purpose, it is time to begin the actual writing process.

In academic writing, you will write in a three-part format:

- Introduction
- Body
- Conclusion

In law enforcement writing, you will follow the same basic pattern, but it is likely that your report will become a part of a larger file, so you don't have to be so concerned about having a formal conclusion.

Writing the Introduction

The introduction should introduce your topic and provide background information moving from general to specific. The introduction will set the tone for the paper and prepare your reader for the information you will be presenting. In academic writing, you might begin with a question, a brief story, or a definition. This is an opportunity to capture your reader's interest, so try to make this part interesting.

The last sentence of your introduction should be your thesis statement, which will express the main idea and map out the body of the paper for your reader. Your thesis statement should be narrow enough to be addressed in the paper. It is important that your thesis statement is not a declaration, a statement of fact, or a broad statement.

Declaration: In this paper, I will argue the merits of racial profiling.

Statement of Fact: Racial profiling is often used by police officers.

Broad Statement: Racial profiling is a controversial issue.

Thesis: Since the terrorist attacks of September 11, racial profiling has become a more accepted screening method for law enforcement agencies.

With this thesis statement, the reader knows that the paper will focus on the effects of the events of September 11 on attitudes towards profiling. From this point, the writer can define racial profiling and compare and contrast attitudes before and after the attacks. The writer might also research and offer theories as to why these attitudes have changed.

In a professional situation, the introduction to an incident report will establish the initial call, date, time of arrival, and observations at the time of arrival. From there, the writer will recount a chronological account of the incident, reporting all relevant information.

Writing the Body

The body of the paper incorporates evidence, definitions, and examples that will support your thesis statement. This is the time to add and drop ideas from your preliminary research and start organizing information into paragraphs.

Each paragraph needs to have a topic sentence, and everything included in that paragraph needs to relate directly to the topic sentence. When you are trying to organize your information, it is a good idea to group your research material into categories; this will help you to determine the topic of each paragraph.

Give some thought to how you want to arrange the paragraphs in the paper. You can organize by using time order (the order in which events happened), space order (the order in which objects are arranged, as in describing the contents of a room), or order of importance (least to most or most to least).

A detailed outline will help you to organize your information, and it will also keep you from straying from the topic. Another benefit of writing a detailed outline is that it lets you see your strong and weak areas. If you see that your outline lacks sufficient development in a particular area, you can start looking for additional information before you are actually in the middle of writing the paper.

Using your outline and research material, you can write your supporting body paragraphs with relative ease.

In professional writing situations, you would recount the events of the investigation in chronological (time) order. The specific information might include observations, actions at the scene, identities of people on the scene, contact and witness information, and specific details obtained from interviewees.

Writing the Conclusion

The conclusion to your paper needs to restate the thesis and summarize the main points. No new information should be introduced in the conclusion. Your conclusion might contain a quotation, a brief story, or a recommendation. Remember that the conclusion is the impression that the reader will take away, so be sure to wrap up all the loose ends and revisit the most important points.

In a professional situation, your conclusion might state what follow-up activities you will conduct for the investigation. If there are no follow-up activities indicated, you will conclude by telling what time you left the scene and, perhaps, how the scene appeared when you left.

The conclusion is really a summary of the major information already covered, so it can be shorter than other sections of the paper.

REVISING

The third major step in the writing process is revising. Many students assume that revising simply means proofreading, but revising is a much more complicated beast than proofreading.

The act of revision should be a thorough one. It is best to walk away from the paper and then look at it again in twenty-four hours or so. By this time you have been away from your writing long enough that you can look at your paper with more objectivity. This is the right time to see if you need to reorder your paragraphs for better impact. You can also look for any weak paragraphs and strengthen them with more detail. Working at a word processor makes this an easy task—you can cut and paste, delete, and insert information.

It is also a good idea to get someone else to read your paper and give you feedback. Someone removed from the task can offer new insights and point out areas that might not be clear or well supported.

After you have taken care of the major revision of the paper, it's time for editing and proofreading. Use a dictionary to look up words you aren't sure about, and run the grammar checker and spell checker from your word processing program. But don't stop with an on-screen reading. Print out a hard copy of the paper and read it aloud, checking for spelling and grammar errors that you missed. If you stumble over a sentence as you read it aloud, there is a good chance that it is awkward or confusing.

Rewrite these sentences so they flow more smoothly. Another good tip for reading aloud is to breathe only where punctuation allows. If you find that you are hyperventilating or running out of air, you might want to do some sentence-length revision.

Next, make the revisions from the hard copy on your computer file and print out the final copy.

In a professional writing situation, you will want to look over your field notes as you review your report. If you find that you have omitted information, add it. Double-check the times to make sure they are in chronological order, and verify specific details such as the spelling of names and the accuracy of social security numbers, dates of birth, telephone numbers, and addresses. Remember that many reports are a matter of public record, and that most libel suits occur because of careless errors.

In Chapter 1, you learned about the seven C's of report writing. As you make your final revisions, make sure that your report includes all of the critical elements.

SUMMARY

Careful planning and organizing can make a difficult writing task much more manageable.

The writing process can be broken into three major parts:

Prewriting

Prewriting provides an opportunity to gather the information needed for writing and includes brainstorming, clustering, and free writing. During the prewriting process, the author must determine the purpose for the writing project and the intended audience.

Writing

The writing stage begins after the writer has gathered information and determined the writing purpose and audience.

The essay is made up of an introduction, which provides background information, and a statement of purpose, or thesis statement. The thesis statement is backed up by specific supporting evidence, which makes up the body of the essay. The final component of the essay is the conclusion, which offers a summary of the information in the essay and a restatement of the thesis.

Revising

Revision is a thorough process involving a major rewrite of the first draft of the paper. During revision the writer should make sure the essay is well organized and supported. Writers should ask other readers for feedback and incorporate changes in the draft.

The final step in revising is proofreading for errors in spelling, punctuation, and mechanics. Writers should proofread both on-screen and with a printed hard copy of the paper.

ACTIVITIES

Assume that you have been asked to write an essay about the lasting effects of the September 11 terrorist attacks.

1. Brainstorm by clustering.
2. Brainstorm by free writing.
3. Create a list of ideas you will include in your essay.
4. Write a thesis statement for your essay.
5. Create an outline for your essay.
6. Write a rough draft of your essay.
7. Write a final draft of your essay.

UNIT II

Writing for Law Enforcement

3

Writing a Law Enforcement Report

SPECIAL CONSIDERATIONS

Writing for law enforcement carries a number of special considerations for the writer. First, the document will become a part of a permanent public record that will be read by a number of different parties. Errors in the report can result in a number of negative consequences, including weakening of the case and humiliation for the writer.

An officer's writing skills can also impact his or her career options. Good writers might get better performance evaluations and promotion opportunities, while poor writers are more likely to be limited by their own writing skills. You must remember that higher-level positions require more administrative duties, including writing and editing subordinates' writing. The ability to carry out these responsibilities will enter into a promotion decision.

WHY WE WRITE

With the special needs of law enforcement writing, it is important to understand the reasons we are writing. We write to:

- Communicate with every reader
- Document an occurrence
- Aid in follow-up activities
- Provide facts for trial
- Document job performance
- Provide statistical data
- Provide reference material

WHAT REPORTS REFLECT

The reports that you write reflect upon you as the writer in a number of ways. From reading your reports, readers will form opinions about you regarding:

Intelligence	Experience
Education	Background
Training	Credibility

What impression are you making?

CRITERIA FOR A GOOD REPORT

A good report must be:

- Correct
- Concise
- Complete
- Clear
- Legible
- Objective
- Grammatically Correct
- Mechanically Correct

Correct

Always verify your information for the final report. Make sure that your information is correct by checking your field notes. You must also ensure that you are providing verifiable information. Be especially careful to double-check spelling and all numbers.

Concise

Remember that you want to use precise language with minimal verbiage. As a professional, you should also use correct terminology and appropriate language in your report.

Complete

Include all information that is relevant to the report you are writing. As an officer, remember that your job is to present the facts, even though they might appear to weaken a case. Do not omit information that may prove to be vital later in the investigation. Keep in mind the *who, what, when, where, why,* and *how* questions, and answer all that are necessary.

Who

Discovered the incident?
Reported the incident?
Witnessed the incident?
Are suspects in the incident?
Can identify offenders?
Can identify property?

Include:

Role—victims, suspects, witnesses, etc.
Full names, spelled correctly
Addresses and phone numbers
Ages and dates of birth
Social Security and Driver's License numbers
Race/Ethnicities
Occupations or schools attended

What

Happened?
Does the victim know?
Can witnesses tell?
Evidence is available?
Was needed to commit the crime?
Was the M.O.?
Events led to the incident?

Include:

Offense—use legal terms
Missing or damaged items
Means of transportation
Statements obtained
Unusual characteristics

When

Did the incident occur?

Include:

Chronology of events

Where

Was the incident committed?
Are possible witnesses?
Are possible suspects?
Was the victim?

Why (motive)

For revenge?
For gain?
An addiction?
An accident?

How

Did the suspects access the crime scene?

These are general considerations for what information should be included in the report. The information that you include will help others to make decisions about what follow-up activities should be implemented, so be as complete as possible.

Clear

Use chronological order to write the narrative. Headings can also be used in the final report to separate sections of the investigation, such as the description of the scene; interviews with witnesses, victims, and suspects; and follow-up activities. Illustrations, such as scene sketches and photographs, can also be included in the report.

Legible

The reader must be able to decipher your writing (even your field notes), so you must be very neat with your handwriting. A good practice for field notes is to print in all capital letters using black ink. If you must make a correction, cross out the omission with one line through the middle of the words (don't scribble out words) and make a neat correction in the margin.

Your final narrative report should be typed. If this is not possible, write a draft of the report on a separate sheet of paper, proofread and make corrections, and then print the final draft using all capital letters.

Objective

Remember that you are acting as an impartial information gatherer and law enforcer in any given situation. You are not an attorney, judge, or juror. Make sure that your writing reflects your role as an officer and is impartial. Do not omit information that appears to weaken the case. Stick to the facts, and do not include any information that cannot be substantiated. Avoid language that might be interpreted as reflecting sexism, racism, or any other bias.

With all of this in mind, let's examine the most common writing task for a law enforcement officer: an incident report. From the officer's point of view, the incident must begin with the initial dispatch to the scene.

From the moment of dispatch, an officer should be making mental and written notes about observations and conditions surrounding the call. For, example, a car speeding away from the direction of the call could later prove to be a vital piece of information in the case. These observations will initially be recorded in the officer's field notes and will later be used to write the official narrative report, which will then be submitted to others for follow-up activities.

FIELD NOTES

A field notebook is an essential tool of the trade for law enforcement. If your department does not have a specific preference for the type of notebook you use, you need to decide what will work best for you. You might select a small spiral-bound notebook or a loose-leaf notebook. Be sure that the notebook you select has a firm enough back to enable you to write while standing and is small enough for you to hold easily in one hand.

The notebook should be used to record your observations at the scene and other relevant information.

Possible Details to Include in Field Notes

Your field notes will act as a reminder of the details in your final written report, so you must be sure to include all relevant information. You will want to begin with a notation of the time and location of the dispatch. You will also need to note your time of arrival and your actions upon arrival. Record your initial observations upon arrival at the scene.

Next, you will probably begin interviewing people present at the scene. Record the interviewees' names (verify spellings), dates of birth, social security numbers, residential addresses and telephone numbers, professions, and places of employment.

Your interview questions will be either closed-ended (yes or no answers such as, "Did you witness the car accident?") or open-ended (requiring a detailed answer such as, "Can you please describe what you saw?"). Take detailed notes about what the interviewee offers as information unless you notice that your writing seems to be making the person hesitant to talk. If this occurs, consider taking only minimal notes.

You can also make sketches of the scene in your field notes, along with technical information such as measurements and other observations. Photographic evidence may also be noted briefly in your notes.

Keep in mind that your field notes may be read by others. Defendants, plaintiffs, defense attorneys, and insurance companies may request your notes and may be granted access. Never make notes that could be used to diminish your credibility later. Although it is appropriate for your notebook to contain personal observations, opinions, comments to yourself, and data that may not be included in the report, absolutely refrain from using your notebook to write your own personal comments such as obscenities, doodles, unprofessional comments, inappropriate jokes, or information that should not be disclosed to the public.

Incident Scene Procedure

Keep in mind that you will need to sift through all the information gathered and the procedures followed at the scene to determine what details should be included in your narrative. Although the procedures you follow will vary from one situation to another, the one constant you will have to deal with is the need to document the incident.

INCIDENT REPORTS

The incident report will include a face page (provided by your agency), narrative continuation pages, interview reports, evidence reports, and supporting materials such as sketches and photographs.

While this task might appear overwhelming for a new recruit, it can be broken down into a series of manageable steps.

The Face Page

Every agency will have its own specific face page for a particular incident. While sample pages are provided in this text (see Figures 3.3 and 3.4), face pages vary significantly from one agency to another, so you will need to find out what form you should use.

The face page will usually consist of standard codified information blanks that need to be filled in. Most agencies have an officer's handbook that specifies the correct coding for various incidents and offenses. You need to familiarize yourself with your agency's handbook so that you will know the particular requirements of your agency.

The face page will usually require standard information, including the incident location, type, and date; party information (victims and witnesses), including names, social security numbers, gender, race, addresses and phone numbers; vehicle information (if indicated), including type, tag number, year, model, VIN, style, color, and distinguishing marks; and the name of the officer who prepared the report, the assisting officers, and the report reviewer.

Use your notes to verify all the information that you include in the face page. Make sure to double-check all information.

The Continuation Page

The narrative section, often referred to as the continuation page, offers further information about the incident. This is the section of the report that will reflect your writing skills, so write this section thoughtfully and carefully.

You will use your field notes to provide the information in this section, which you will write in chronological order and in past tense. The narrative will usually begin with the time of dispatch, followed by the time of arrival at the scene. Then, you will provide an accounting of the observations you made upon arrival at the scene, the actions you took, and any events that occurred while you were responding to the incident. Remember that the purpose of the narrative is to record information that is not covered in the face page.

Use chronological order. Chronological order describes events in the order in which they happened. When you are describing a sequence of events, it is best to report them from your point of view, from the beginning. For example, if you are responding to a domestic violence call, you will report the events from your point of view, beginning with the dispatch call. Next you will note your time of arrival at the scene and begin an accounting of your observations and actions on site in the order in which they occurred. If you have taken good field notes, you should be able to easily separate the events into chronological order.

Use specific time markers. Your agency will specify what type of time you should use. Many agencies use military time. If you do not have a specific time for an event, you can use an approximation, as long as you indicate clearly that the time is approximated.

Write in past tense. By the time you write the narrative, you will be recounting events that have already happened. It is important to write in the past tense and to stay in the past tense unless you are suggesting follow-up activities for the future. A common pitfall for writers is to slip into the present tense when the recounted action becomes exciting, so be sure that you have not slipped out of past tense.

Write in first person if your agency allows it. There was a time when law enforcement officers were encouraged to use the third person voice to refer to themselves. It was commonly held that the third person referral to one's self assisted in maintaining a sense of objectivity. Using third person voice means that you refer to yourself by your name or "this officer," instead of referring to yourself in the first person, "I." For example, "This officer arrived at the scene at 0900 hours." More recently, agencies have moved to a first person accounting in the narrative section, primarily because it has proven to be less confusing. Some agencies still prefer the third person narrative voice, so check with your supervisor and use the preferred voice.

Avoid bias in your writing. Remember that you are an impartial party in the case, so do not show any bias or opinion in the narrative. You can offer observations with supporting evidence, but avoid making judgmental statements. For example, do not say that a driver was intoxicated. Instead, you might say that the driver appeared to be impaired and offer the details that led you to this conclusion: slurred speech, impaired coordination, watery eyes, and the presence of an odor that might be associated with consumption of an alcoholic beverage. This information avoids making a judgment and describes the conditions that might lead to a field sobriety test or other actions.

Use headings to separate sections. Headings can be useful as an organizational tool for both readers and the writer. Remember that readers are reading for a specific purpose, and that they are looking for specific information. Separating the narrative into sections labeled by headings will help you organize the narrative so that you are not trying to address everything at once. Also, readers will find information more quickly by being able to read the headings and then read the specific information they need. Headings should be flush left and written in all capital letters. The body of the section should begin on the next line. If you were investigating a breaking and entering incident, you might select the following headings:

ARRIVAL OBSERVATIONS	VICTIM INTERVIEW
METHOD OF ENTRY	WITNESS INTERVIEW
ITEMS MISSING	FOLLOW-UP ACTIVITIES

Avoid repetition and wordiness. You don't have to repeat the same information in every section of the narrative. Repetition tires and irritates the reader. You should also eliminate any wordy phrases and passive voice so that the writing is concise and clear.

Proofread your narrative carefully. Even if you are using a word processing computer program with a spellchecker, you still need to proofread for errors. Use your field notes, agency handbooks, dictionaries, telephone books, maps, and any other resource material that will help you. While on-screen proofreading is useful, always print a hard copy of the narrative for a second proofreading. Writers often miss errors unless they have the paper copy to review. It is always a good idea to have a second reader, so you might want to have a more experienced officer look at your narrative and offer suggestions for improvement.

Take constructive criticism gracefully. If you are in the early stages of your career, chances are that you will be asked to revise your narrative. Remember that these suggestions are offered in a helpful spirit, so don't become defensive. Keep in mind that you are writing a professional narrative report that could be used by many different individuals and agencies, so this is really a team project. In many cases there will be nothing really wrong with the narrative you have written, but supervisors might have different style preferences for you to use. Always keep in mind that you are writing a professional report narrative—not the great American novel. Make the suggested changes, remember the stylistic preferences for the next report, and go on about your business.

Follow-Up Reports

Any incident requiring further action will result in a follow-up report, which is also written in narrative form. This report should follow all the rules of a narrative report, and it may also become public record. In the follow-up report, use chronological order and past tense, and include all relevant information.

The follow-up may require a brief introduction providing a summary of the initial incident. You will also want to include any information that has been discovered since the initial report. Follow-up reports might describe the conditions and events surrounding the recovery of stolen items, witnesses who were interviewed away from the scene, or further developments surrounding the incident.

Supplemental Materials

Supplemental materials are attachments for inclusion in the case file. These materials may be drawings, photographs, statements, waivers, warrants, lab reports, or evidence reports. You may have to provide a chain of custody for evidence, and it may be included in this section. Some departments will have specific forms for this information, while others simply include these documents as appendices or as separate documents. Familiarize yourself with your agency's policy about these materials.

Clinton Police Department
401 Gary Blvd Clinton, OK 73601

Narrative

Report Date	Type of Incident	Complaint No.	Status	Page
07/02/2003	BURGLARY (RESIDENCE DURING DAY)	2003-0630	OPEN	1

Narrative:

ON 07-02-03, AT APPROXIMATELY 10:11 A.M., I WAS DISPATCHED TO ▓▓▓▓▓▓, IN REFERENCE TO A RESIDENTIAL BURGLARY. UPON MY ARRIVAL, I MET WITH THE VICTIM, ▓▓▓ ▓▓▓▓▓, AND HIS FATHER, ▓▓▓▓▓▓▓▓. ▓▓▓▓▓▓ TOLD ME THAT HE AND HIS WIFE, LINDA ▓▓▓▓▓, ARRIVED HOME ON 07-02-03 AT APPROXIMATELY 9:40 A.M. HE LIVES AT 123 ▓▓▓▓▓ AVENUE. ▓▓▓ SAID THAT HE SAW A GRAY 4 DOOR CAR, LICENSE PLATE/▓▓▓▓▓, PARKED IN FRONT OF HIS SON'S HOUSE AT ▓▓▓ NORTH 2ND. ▓▓▓ SAID THAT HE ASKED THE OCCUPANT OF THE CAR WHAT HE WAS DOING. HE TOLD ▓▓▓ THAT HIS FRIEND WAS THERE LOOKING FOR ANOTHER FRIEND. ▓▓▓ ASKED HIM WHAT HIS NAME WAS AND HE REPLIED, "FRED JONES". THE PERSON WAS A WHITE MALE, APPROXIMATELY 6FT TALL, HIS HEAD WAS SHAVED AND HE HAD A WHITE TEE SHIRT ON. EARL SAW THAT THE DOOR TO HIS SON'S HOUSE WAS OPEN AND HE KNEW THAT HIS SON WAS AT WORK. ▓▓▓ WENT INTO HIS SON'S HOUSE TO SEE WHAT WAS GOING ON, BUT HE DIDN'T FIND ANYONE INSIDE. ▓▓▓ SAID THAT HIS WIFE CALLED OUT TO HIM AND HE RAN OUTSIDE AND SAW ANOTHER WHITE MALE GETTING INTO THE GRAY CAR. ▓▓▓ DESCRIBED THE SECOND WHITE MALE AS BEING APPROXIMATELY 5FT 7IN TO 5FT 9IN TALL, 150 POUNDS, BLACK HAIR, WEARING A BLACK SHIRT AND HAD HIS LOWER LIP PIERCED. THE SECOND MALE GOT INTO THE CAR AND NEARLY HIT LINDA WITH THE CAR. ▓▓▓ SAID THAT THE WHITE MALE SPED AWAY NORTHBOUND ON 2ND STREET. I OBTAINED A WRITTEN STATEMENT FROM ▓▓▓. (SEE STATEMENT).

▓▓▓ TOLD ME THAT HE LOCKED HIS FRONT DOOR AND LEFT HIS RESIDENCE ON 07-02-03 AT APPROXIMATELY 6:30 A.M. TO GO TO WORK. HE SAID THAT HIS MOTHER CALLED HIM ON 07-02-03 AT APPROXIMATELY 9:50 A.M. AND TOLD HIM THAT SOMEONE HAD BROKEN INTO HIS HOUSE. ▓▓▓ SAID THAT HE SAW THAT HIS FRONT DOOR HAD BEEN PRYED OPEN. ▓▓▓ LOOKED INSIDE HIS HOUSE AND FOUND THAT HIS DVD SURROUND SOUND SYSTEM AND HIS 8 INCH DIAMETER TELESCOPE HAD BEEN STOLEN. ▓▓▓ SAID THAT THE SUSPECTS LEFT BEHIND 2 OF THE SMALLER SPEAKERS TO THE SYSTEM. ▓▓▓ SAID THAT THE SYSTEM WAS A PHILLIPS BRAND, MODEL/MX 3600 D3701, SERIAL NUMBER/7217466 AND VALUED AT APPROXIMATELY $400.00. ▓▓▓ SAID THAT HE DIDN'T KNOW THE BRAND OF THE TELESCOPE, BUT IT IS 8 INCH DIAMETER AND VALUED AT APPROXIMATELY $800.00. ▓▓▓ FOUND A GLASS BOWL LYING IN THE LIVING ROOM THAT HE KEPT SPARE CHANGE IN. THE CHANGE WAS STOLEN. ▓▓▓ SAID THAT HE DOESN'T KNOW WHO THE SUSPECTS COULD HAVE BEEN. I OBTAINED A WRITTEN STATEMENT FROM ▓▓▓. (SEE STATEMENT).

I SAW THAT THE FRONT (SOUTH) DOOR HAD PRY MARKS ON IT, WHICH COULD HAVE BEEN CAUSED BY A SCREWDRIVER, PRYBAR OR SIMILAR INSTRUMENT. I TOOK PHOTOS OF THE DOOR AND THEY ARE SAVED IN THE IMAGES SECTION OF THIS REPORT. I SEIZED THE GLASS BOWL AS EVIDENCE. I PLACED IT IN A PAPER SACK AND LATER TAGGED IT AND PLACED IT IN AN EVIDENCE LOCKER AT THE POLICE DEPARTMENT. I LATER HAD DISPATCH ENTER THE SURROUND SOUND SYSTEM INTO N.C.I.C.

WHILE I WAS AT ▓▓▓ RESIDENCE, I GAVE THE DESCRIPTION OF THE SUSPECTS AND THE GRAY CAR TO SGT. SCOTT GOODMAN, WHO WAS ALSO ON DUTY. THE LICENSE PLATE ON THE CAR THAT ▓▓▓ GAVE ME, ▓▓▓, SHOWED TO BE REGISTERED TO ▓▓▓ OR ▓▓▓, ▓▓▓, CLINTON, OK. SGT. GOODMAN WAS UNABLE TO LOCATE THE CAR OR SUSPECTS, BUT HE TALKED TO ▓▓▓, WHO IS ▓▓▓ MOTHER. ▓▓▓ TOLD SGT. GOODMAN THAT BRYAN WAS IN A REHAB FACILITY AND THAT HE HAD SOLD THE CAR TO ▓▓▓

ON 07-02-03, AT APPROXIMATELY 12:30 P.M., I MET WITH LINDA ▓▓▓ AT HER PLACE OF

Reporting Officer MCADAMS, JEFF # 5	Approving Officer #5 07/02/2003 MCADAMS, JEFF (I)

Figure 3.1. Good narrative report. Provided courtesy of Chief Edward Smith, Clinton Police Department, Clinton, OK.

Clinton Police Department

401 Gary Blvd Clinton, OK 73601

Narrative

Report Date	Type of Incident	Complaint No.	Status	Page
07/02/2003	**BURGLARY (RESIDENCE DURING DAY)**	2003-0630	**OPEN**	2

EMPLOYMENT. LINDA TOLD ME THAT ON 07-02-03, AT APPROXIMATELY 9:30 A.M., SHE AND HER HUSBAND, ████████████████, ARRIVED HOME AT 123 ████████ AVENUE. SHE AND ████ SAW A WHITE MALE COME OUT OF THEIR SON'S YARD AT 311 NORTH 2ND. THE WHITE MALE WAS CARRYING SOMETHING AND PUT IT INTO A GRAY 4 DOOR CAR WITH OKLAHOMA LICENSE PLATE/████, WHICH WAS PARKED IN FRONT OF THEIR SON'S HOUSE. LINDA SAID THAT ████ GOT OUT AND TALKED TO THE WHITE MALE, WHO TOLD ████ THAT HE AND HIS BUDDY WERE VISITING A FRIEND. LINDA AND EARL KNEW THAT THEIR SON WAS AT WORK. LINDA SAID THAT ████ WENT INTO THEIR SON'S HOUSE. SHE SAID THAT THE WHITE MALE WAS PROBABLY IN HIS 20'S, HIS HEAD WAS SHAVED AND HE HAD ON A WHITE TEE SHIRT WITH WRITING ON IT. LINDA SAID THAT WHEN ████ WENT INTO THE HOUSE, THE WHITE MALE RAN WEST DOWN THE ALLEY. LINDA SAID THAT A SECOND WHITE MALE CAME WALKING UP TO THE GRAY CAR, FROM SOMEWHERE AROUND THE HOUSES. LINDA SAID THAT SHE STOOD IN FRONT OF THE GRAY CAR AND TOLD THE SECOND WHITE MALE NOT TO MOVE THE CAR. LINDA SAID THAT HE DROVE THE CAR TOWARD HER AND SHE MOVED AS HE DROVE AWAY. LINDA SAID THAT THE SECOND MALE WAS PROBABLY IN HIS 20'S. HE HAD BLACK HAIR AND WAS WEARING A BLACK SHIRT AND BLACK PANTS. HE ALSO HAD HIS LOWER LIP PIERCED WITH A STUD. I OBTAINED A WRITTEN STATEMENT FROM LINDA. (SEE STATEMENT).

Reporting Officer MCADAMS, JEFF # 5	Approving Officer #5 07/02/2003 MCADAMS, JEFF (I)

Figure 3.1.   (*Continued*)

Clinton Police Department
401 Gary Blvd Clinton, OK 73601

Narrative

Report Date	Type of Incident	Complaint No.	Status	Page
09/10/2002	THEFT $200 UP (ALL OTHER)	2002-0808	UNF	1

Narrative:

    ON 09-10-02 AT APPROXIMATELY 1931 HOURS I WAS DISPATCHED TO ▬▬ SOUTH 25TH STREET IN CLINTON OKLAHOMA, IN REFERENCE OF A STOLEN HONDA LAWN MOWER.

    UPON ARRIVAL, I MADE CONTACT WITH ▬▬▬▬▬▬▬ ADVISED ME THAT ON 09-02-02 SOMETIME IN THE MORNING SHE WAS GOING TO MOW THE LAWN WHEN SHE NOTICED THAT HER RED HONDA COMMERCIAL PUSH LAWN MOWER WAS MISSING. ▬▬ HAD THE LAWN MOWER BEHIND HER WAVE RUNNER IN FRONT OF THE HOUSE. ▬▬ NOTICED THE LAWN MOWER THERE ON 08-31-02 SOMETIME IN THE MORNING.

    ▬▬ DON'T KNOW WHO COULD OF STOLEN THE LAWN MOWER. ▬▬ ADVISED ME THAT THE LAWN MOWER WAS VALUED AT APPROXIMATELY $1000.00.

    I OBTAINED A WRITTEN STATEMENT FROM ▬▬▬▬, WHICH IS ATTACHED TO MY REPORT.

Reporting Officer GONZALES, MIGUEL # 14	Approving Officer

Figure 3.2. Poor narrative report. Provided courtesy of Chief Edward Smith, Clinton Police Department, Clinton, OK.

NON-FATALITY TRAFFIC ACCIDENTS

Traffic accident reports that do not involve a fatality include very little narrative. Your department will have accident forms and you will fill out the appropriate information in the provided space. This allows for more efficient reporting at the scene of the accident so that traffic can begin moving as quickly as possible.

Once you have arrived at the scene, you will assess the situation, call for medical assistance if needed, set up traffic flow, and begin interviewing the drivers, passengers, and witnesses.

From the information you observe and gather, you will draw a diagram in the space provided and write a brief narrative describing what you observe at the scene. Remember to be brief in this narrative.

FATALITY TRAFFIC ACCIDENTS

When you work a traffic accident involving a fatality, the need for strong narrative becomes critical. First, if driver negligence, alcohol, or drug use were involved, criminal charges may be filed against one or more of the drivers. Second, insurance companies will want detailed information for claim settlement investigations. Finally, civil litigation may occur as a result of the accident. Because of the gravity of a fatal accident, a thorough investigation must follow, and you must document this investigation.

At the scene of the accident, you will use the forms provided by your department to record the details of the accident, including diagrams and brief narrative. You will also want to record the names and contact information of any witnesses so you can interview them later.

After working the initial accident, you will need to interview passengers in the vehicles, witnesses to the accident, and emergency personnel who worked the scene.

You will then write an extended narrative report, recounting the information gathered in each interview. Be sure to separate each interview and identify the person being interviewed. You should also give the details surrounding the interview—was it in person? Where? Was it conducted by phone? Was the conversation recorded? What time did the interview occur? What information did the interviewee offer?

Finally, you will need to obtain a copy of the medical examiner's report for inclusion in the case file.

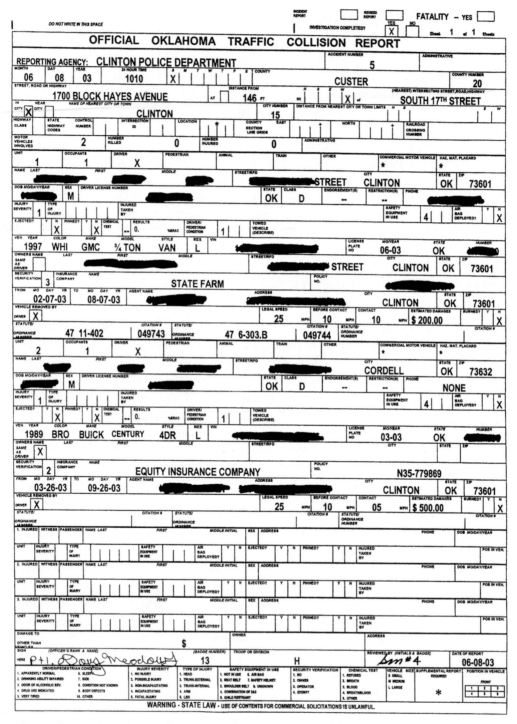

Figure 3.3. Sample non-fatality traffic accident. Provided courtesy of Chief Edward Smith, Clinton Police Department, Clinton, OK.

Case Number 5

REMARKS

UNIT 1 WAS WEST BOUND IN THE 1700 BLOCK OF HAYES AVENUE. UNIT 2 WAS EAST BOUND IN THE 1700 BLOCK OF HAYES AVENUE. UNIT 1 ATTEMPTED TO TURN LEFT INTO AN ALLEY AND FAILED TO YIELD THE RIGHT OF WAY TO UNIT 2. DRIVER OF UNIT 2 BRAKED TO AVOID A COLLISION. THE FRONT BUMPER OF UNIT 1 COLLIDED WITH THE FRONT BUMPER OF UNIT 2. POINT OF IMPACT WAS APPROXIMATELY 7 FEET NORTH OF THE SOUTH EDGE OF HAYES AVENUE AND APPROXIMATELY 146 FEET WEST OF THE EAST EDGE OF SOUTH 17TH STREET.

BLK	REMARKS UNIT 1	BLK	REMARKS UNIT 2
1	FAILED TO YIELD RIGHT OF WAY WHEN TURNING LEFT	8	NO IMPROPER ACTION

THIS REPORT IS BASED ON THE OFFICER'S INVESTIGATION OF THIS ACCIDENT. IT MAY CONTAIN THE OPINION OF THE OFFICER

Figure 3.3. (*Continued*)

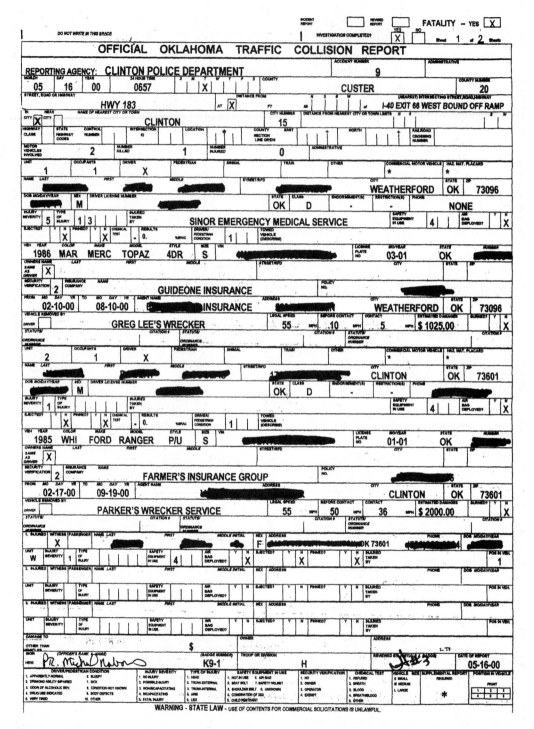

Figure 3.4. Sample fatality traffic accident. Provided courtesy of Chief Edward Smith, Clinton Police Department, Clinton, OK.

Case Number 9

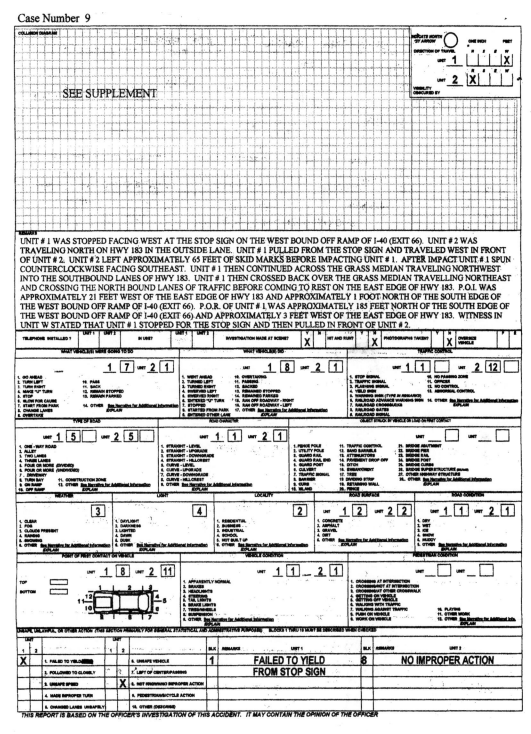

Figure 3.4. *(Continued)*

[*DO NOT WRITE IN THIS SPACE*   ]   Sheet 2 of 2 Sheets

OFFICIAL OKLAHOMA TRUCK AND BUS COLLISION REPORT -- SUPPLEMENT

WHEN TO USE THIS FORM: *Did the collision involve ....*

PART 1
A truck with at least two axles and six tires? .... Y Ⓝ
Any vehicle with a hazardous material placard? .... Y Ⓝ
A bus designed to carry 15 or more persons, including the driver? .... Y Ⓨ

STOP! *If any response to Part 1 is "YES" continue to PART 2. If all responses to PART 1 are "NO" do not complete this form.*

PART 2
Any person who was fatally injured? .... Ⓨ N
Any injured person requiring transport for immediate medical treatment? .... Y Ⓝ
One or more vehicles that had to be towed from the scene as a result of the collision? ..... Ⓨ N
One or more vehicles that required repair or were provided assistance before proceeding from the scene under own power? .... Ⓨ Ⓝ

STOP! *If any response to Part 2 is "YES" complete this form. If all responses to PART 2 are "NO" do not complete this form.*

TRUCK/BUS/HAZ MAT VEH		CONTINUATION		REPORTING AGENCY			ACCIDENT NO.		ADMINISTRATIVE
X				CLINTON POLICE DEPARTMENT			9		

MONTH	DAY	YEAR	24 HOUR TIME	COUNTY				COUNTY NUMBER
05	16	00	0657		CUSTER			20

UNIT NUMBER		US DOT CENSUS NUMBER		ICC NUMBER

CARRIER NUMBER			SAME AS DRIVER	SAME AS OWNER	SOURCE OF CARRIER NAME

CARRIER ADDRESS	STREET/RFD	CITY	STATE	ZIP

GVWR/GCWR	TOTAL NO. AXLES	HAZ MAT PLACARD	Y	N	MATERIAL IDENTIFICATION NUMBER	HAZARD CLASS	HAZARDOUS MATERIAL SPILL	Y	N	TOWED	Y	N

EVENT 1	EVENT 2	EVENT 3	EVENT 4	ACCESS CONTROL	TRAFFICWAY	VEHICLE CONFIGURATION	CARGO BODY TYPE

SEQUENCE OF EVENTS (UP TO FOUR EVENTS)	ACCESS CONTROL	TRAFFICWAY
1. RAN OFF ROAD 2. JACKKNIFE 3. OVERTURN (ROLLOVER) 4. DOWNHILL RUNAWAY 5. CARGO LOSS OR SHIFT 6. EXPLOSION 7. SEPARATION OF UNITS COLLISION INVOLVING 8. PEDESTRIAN 9. MOTOR VEHICLE IN TRANSPORT 10. PARKED MOTOR VEHICLE 11. TRAIN 12. PEDALCYCLE 13. ANIMAL 14. FIXED OBJECT 15. OTHER OBJECT 16. OTHER EVENT	1. NO CONTROL (UNLIMITED ACCESS) 2. FULL CONTROL (ONLY RAMP ENTRY AND EXIT) 3. OTHER	1. NOT PHYSICALLY DIVIDED 2-WAY TRAFFICWAY 2. DIVIDED HIGHWAY, MEDIAN STRIP WITHOUT TRAFFIC BARRIER 3. DIVIDED HIGHWAY, MEDIAN STRIP WITH TRAFFIC BARRIER 4. ONE-WAY TRAFFICWAY

VEHICLE CONFIGURATION   CARGO BODY TYPE

INJURED/WITNESS CONTINUATION

4	INJURED	WITNESS	PASSENGER	NAME LAST	FIRST	MI	SEX	ADDRESS	PHONE	DOB MO/DAY/YR
UNIT	INJ SEV	TYPE OF INJ		SAFETY EQUIP IN USE	AIR BAG DEPLOYED	Y N	EJECTED Y N	PINNED Y N	INJURED TAKEN BY	POS IN VEH

5	INJURED	WITNESS	PASSENGER	NAME LAST	FIRST	MI	SEX	ADDRESS	PHONE	DOB MO/DAY/YR
UNIT	INJ SEV	TYPE OF INJ		SAFETY EQUIP IN USE	AIR BAG DEPLOYED	Y N	EJECTED Y N	PINNED Y N	INJURED TAKEN BY	POS IN VEH

6	INJURED	WITNESS	PASSENGER	NAME LAST	FIRST	MI	SEX	ADDRESS	PHONE	DOB MO/DAY/YR
UNIT	INJ SEV	TYPE OF INJ		SAFETY EQUIP IN USE	AIR BAG DEPLOYED	Y N	EJECTED Y N	PINNED Y N	INJURED TAKEN BY	POS IN VEH

7	INJURED	WITNESS	PASSENGER	NAME LAST	FIRST	MI	SEX	ADDRESS	PHONE	DOB MO/DAY/YR
UNIT	INJ SEV	TYPE OF INJ		SAFETY EQUIP IN USE	AIR BAG DEPLOYED	Y N	EJECTED Y N	PINNED Y N	INJURED TAKEN BY	POS IN VEH

INJURY SEVERITY	TYPE OF INJURY	SAFETY EQUIPMENT IN USE	POSITION IN VEHICLE	SOURCE OF CARRIER NAME	INVESTIGATOR'S INITIALS & BADGE	DATE	REPORT DATE
1. NO INJURY 2. POSSIBLE INJURY 3. NON-INCAPACITATING 4. INCAPACITATING 5. FATAL INJURY	1. HEAD 2. TRUNK – EXTERNAL 3. TRUNK – INTERNAL 4. ARM 5. LEG	1. NOT IN USE 2. SEAT BELT 3. SHOULDER BELT 4. COMBINATION OF 2 & 3 5. CHILD RESTRAINT 6. AIR BAG 7. SAFETY HELMET	FRONT 1 2 3 4 5 6	1. VEHICLE 2. PAPERS 3. DRIVER 4. LOG BOOK	MN K9-1 REVIEWER'S INITIALS & BADGE H#3	05-17-00 DATE 5/26/00	05/16/00

DPS:0192-02 Rev. 5/97

Figure 3.4.   *(Continued)*

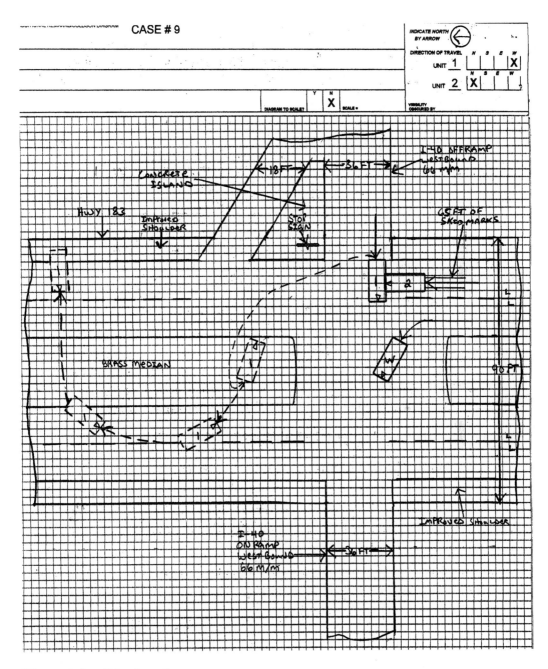

Figure 3.4. (*Continued*)

SEARCH WARRANTS

Obtaining a search warrant is comprised of a three-step process involving the affidavit for search warrant, the search warrant, and the search warrant return. When you ask a judge to issue a search warrant, you must build a probable cause case showing that there is sufficient evidence to justify the search.

Affidavit for Search Warrant

The affidavit for a search warrant is a document that recounts, in narrative form, the information that is being used to justify the issuance of a warrant. In the affidavit for a search warrant, you must establish probable cause to search, and offer evidence that the property is subject to seizure by statute because it is evidence of crime or it was obtained by the fruits of crime.

You will base the affidavit narrative on the most compelling evidence from your investigation narrative reports and your field notes. Be sure to use specific information to support your request for the warrant.

Make sure to double-check all of your facts when you are writing an affidavit for a search warrant. One mistake can cost you the case. Essentially, you are providing the judge with a summary of the events and evidence that lead up to the request for a search warrant.

You will find an example of an affidavit for a search warrant in Figure 3.5. Pay special attention to the detail that is used to justify the request.

The officer begins by establishing his own credibility as a police officer by stating his credentials, affiliation, years of affiliation, and his jurisdictional area.

Having established his credibility, the officer goes on to offer a detailed chronology of the events leading up to the affidavit. The information is clear, concise, and specific and summarizes all of the relevant information.

The Search Warrant

Once you have established probable cause in your affidavit for a search warrant, you must write the actual search warrant.

Because the warrant is not unlimited, you must define the terms of the search by specifying the place to be searched and the items to be searched for. Your search will be limited to the addresses and items you list, so be sure to be inclusive. Remember that you have established probable cause in the narrative section of your affidavit for a search warrant, so make sure to specify only those places and items that have been addressed in the affidavit.

Listing items or locations in the warrant that have not been addressed in the affidavit will raise questions about probable cause and may cause the judge to balk at issuing your warrant. Check the affidavit to make sure you are justified in requesting the specifics on the warrant. If you have presented sufficient evidence of probable cause in your affidavit, the judge will issue the search warrant.

See Figure 3.6 for an example of a search warrant.

IN THE DISTRICT COURT IN AND FOR OKLAHOMA COUNTY

STATE OF OKLAHOMA
STATE OF OKLAHOMA   }
                           }§
COUNTY OF CANADIAN}
AFFIDAVIT FOR SEARCH WARRANT

Lt. Ken W. Brown, affiant, being first duly sworn on oath, deposes and says:

1) I am a commissioned peace officer employed by the El Reno Police Department and have been so employed for Twenty years. I currently hold the rank of Lieutenant. In the course of my employment, I am assigned to investigate actions committed within the city limits of El Reno, County of Canadian, State of Oklahoma, that are contrary to the laws of the State Of Oklahoma.

2) On July 26, 2001 at approximately 1400 hours, Officer Tami Roberts of the El Reno Police Department was radio dispatched to (address) on a possible stolen vehicle. Upon arrival, Officer Roberts met with reporting party, Joe Red the owner of the residence at 206 S. Avenue. Mr. Red told Officer Roberts that Debbie Pink had moved from the residence of 206 S. Street approximately two weeks prior. Mr. Red further stated he had received a notice from the City of El Reno concerning the condition of the property and went over to investigate. Mr. Red met with Jason Blue (aka Jason Pink). Mr. Red noticed a blue in color pickup backed into the garage located at the northwest end of the residence drive way. Mr. Red noted the motor was missing from the vehicle as well as the windshield had been busted out. Mr. Red asked Jason Blue about the missing motor and was told his brother (James Blue aka James Pink) took the motor out of the pickup and placed it in his (James Blue) vehicle.

3) Officer Roberts checked the vehicle and found that the VIN (vehicle identification plate) had been removed or destroyed from the dashboard but found the VIN number affixed to the driver side door. Upon checking the VIN number with Police Headquarters, Officer Roberts learned the vehicle was reported stolen on April 26, 2001 from the El Reno Auto Auction. Officer Roberts was further aware that James Blue (aka Pink) had been arrested earlier in the year for burglary from an auto and learned he was residing at 525 S. Avenue. Officer McBee drove by the reported address and observed James Blue vehicle parked on the north side of the residence at 525 S. Avenue. This information was radioed back to Officer Roberts and Sgt. Hoehner who had arrived to assist Officer Roberts.

4) At approximately 1430 hours, I was contacted by Sgt. Hoehner and was advised of the information received by Officer Roberts. Sgt. Hoehner further stated several bicycles were also found inside of the garage with the stolen truck, which had been reported stolen. I responded to 206 S. Street where I observed the stolen vehicle. The front of the

Figure 3.5.   Search warrant affidavit. Provided courtesy of Captain Joe Stanley, El Reno Police Department, El Reno, OK.

vehicle was facing east toward the open garage doors. The motor and transmission had been removed as well as all four tires, hood, fan shroud and two front fenders.

5) At approximately 1455 hours, Sgt. Hoehner and I went to 525 S. Street. Upon arrival I observed a small white S10 Chevrolet Pickup tag # MMM-MMM Ok/2001, parked on the north side of 525 S. Street and further saw that the hood to the vehicle was up. I then made contact with James Blue. I asked Blue if the small white Pickup belonged to him and Blue stated it did. I asked Mr. Blue for permission to look at his vehicle. Mr. Blue granted permission and accompanied me to the north side of the residence. Mr. Blue stated the vehicle was not running because it had caught fire a few days ago. I asked Mr. Blue what size motor was in the vehicle and he stated a 305cc. Mr. Blue stated he purchased the motor from a friend of his, Jason Brown. According to Blue, Brown purchased the motor from one of his friends, which Blue did not know. Blue further asked what the problem was and then asked if it was related to the vehicle in his old garage on S. Avenue. I asked Blue if he would accompany me to Police Headquarters to talk about the vehicle in the garage on S. Avenue and Blue agreed to do so. Sgt. Hoehner took digital photographs of the motor found in Blue S10 Chevrolet pickup. While I was speaking with James Blue, Sgt. Hoehner spoke to Jason Blue. Sgt. Hoehner further found another completed vehicle motor in the back yard of 525 S. Street. Sgt. Hoehner received the motor number off of the vehicle (GM 3970010). I transported James Blue to Police Headquarters for questioning.

6) At approximately 1515 hours, I interviewed James Blue at Police Headquarters. Mr. Blue stated he purchased the pickup in the garage at 206 S. Avenue from Jason Brown for two hundred dollars. Blue claimed Brown purchased the pickup from someone in Minco and he (Blue) bought the truck three to four months ago for the fenders and bed. Blue stated he had another friend who wanted the pickup bed / fenders and Blue was to finish and repaint them. I asked Blue if he had the title to the pickup in the garage on S. Avenue and Blue stated he bought the truck from Brown without a title and Brown bought it from the person in Minco without a title. I asked Mr. Blue where he had purchased the small white Chevrolet pickup. Blue stated he bought the truck from Candie Yellow. After the interview, Blue was transported back to his residence at 525 S. Street.

7) On 7/27/01 at approximately 1005 hrs, Sgt. Hoehner met with Ronald Purple of 529 S. Street. Mr. Purple told Sgt. Hoehner that James Blue had stolen several vehicle parts from him over the last few months. Purple further stated James Blue admitted to stealing a 1992 Chevrolet pickup from Edmond and further used his shop (1201 S. Place) to pull the motor from his (Blue) S10 Chevrolet pickup and replace it with the motor from the stolen pickup. Purple stated Blue came to his shop wanting to borrow a motor jack. When Purple would not allow the jack to leave his business (Total Service Station), Purple allowed James and Jason Blue to use his shop to install the stolen motor into the white Chevrolet S10. Purple further pointed out the four (4)-cylinder engine block and transmission that James Blue pulled out of his Chevrolet S10 that was lying beside of

Figure 3.5. (*Continued*)

Purple business. Mr. Purple further turned over to Sgt. Hoehner two Chevrolet fenders that James Blue told Purple came from the stolen pickup. Blue wanted Purple to sell the fenders to one of his customers. When the customer (Gary Davis 126 N. "O") learned the fenders were stolen, Davis did not want them. Blue left the fenders at Purple business. Mr. Purple further stated on 7/26/01 he (Purple) went to 525 S. Street and recovered a motor carburetor from Blue white S10 pickup that had been stolen from a vehicle that was parked at his (Purple) business (Total Service Station 1201 S. Place). Mr. Purple turned the recovered carburetor over to Sgt. Hoehner who recognized the carburetor as being similar to the carburetor found on Blue' S10 pickup on 7/26/01 while Officers were at his (Blue') residence.

8) The residence is located within El Reno, Canadian County and the State of Oklahoma with a mailing address of 525 S. Street Ave and found to be a single story wood frame residence painted orange in color with the front door facing west. The residence can further be found as the third house north of Pine Str. on the east side of Street Ave. The vehicle is described as a 1989 Chevrolet S14 VIN #, displaying Oklahoma license number MMM-MMM Ok/2001. The vehicle is parked on the north side of 525 S. Street Ave under the carport.

9) The purpose of the search warrant is to obtain physical evidence such as, photographs, retrieval of the motor serial number to be compared with the number issued from the vehicle manufacture (Chevrolet) by whatever means necessary to allow access to the motor identification number. The 1989 Chevrolet S14 (VIN #) will be transported from 525 S. Street to the City of El Reno maintenance shop for the examination and held until proper identification can be made.

Based upon the above stated facts, your affiant, Lt. Ken W. Brown, request a search warrant be issued by the Judge of the District Court for the above described evidence and for the seizure of the above named or described location.

_____

Affiant

Sworn to before me and subscribed in my presence on this _____ day of _____ 2001.

_____

JUDGE OF THE DISTRICT COURT

Figure 3.5. (*Continued*)

IN THE DISTRICT COURT OF CANADIAN COUNTY

STATE OF OKLAHOMA
THE STATE OF OKLAHOMA

NO. _____

CANADIAN COUNTY

SEARCH WARRANT
IN THE NAME AND AUTHORITY OF THE STATE OF OKLAHOMA,

TO ANY SHERIFF, POLICE OFFICER, OR PEACE OFFICER IN THE COUNTY OF CANADIAN, STATE OF OKLAHOMA.

GREETINGS:

Whereas, Probable cause having been shown on this date before me, by Affiant Lt. Ken W. Brown, of the El Reno Police Department, for believing the following vehicle and things particularly described as follows, to wit:

Photographs, retrieval of the motor serial number to be compared with the number issued from the vehicle manufacture (Chevrolet) by whatever means necessary to allow access to the motor identification number

The residence is located within El Reno, Canadian County and the State of Oklahoma with a mailing address of 525 S. Street Ave and found to be a single story wood frame residence painted white in color with the front door facing west. The residence can further be found as the third house north of Pine Str. on the east side of Street Ave. The vehicle is described as a 1989 Chevrolet S14 VIN # , displaying Oklahoma license number MMM-MMM Ok/2001. The vehicle is parked on the north side of 525 S. Street Ave under the carport

And that the said property is subject to seizure as evidence of a criminal violation of the Statutes of this State pursuant to Oklahoma State Statute Title 21 Section 701.7A.

You are therefore commanded, at any time day or night to make an immediate search of the above-described property for the property described above, and to make a return of this warrant to me, at my office at the Canadian County Courthouse, El Reno, Canadian County, Oklahoma or before a magistrate who presides in the judicial district in which the property was found and seized within 10 (ten) days. You are further commanded to deliver a copy of this warrant to the persons found in possession of the above property or at the place where the warrant is served.

Nighttime service (is authorized) (is not authorized).

Date this _____ day of _____, 2001.

_____ Judge of the District Court,
                                     In and For Canadian County,
                                     The State of Oklahoma.

Figure 3.6.   Search warrant. Provided courtesy of Captain Joe Stanley, El Reno Police Department, El Reno, OK.

Search Warrant Return

The search warrant return is a brief document that acknowledges the seizure of the items specified in the search warrant. It is made up of a statement of who executed the warrant and what items have been inventoried.

See Figure 3.7 for an example of a search warrant return.

SEARCH WARRANT
RETURN

I, Lt. Ken W. Brown, the officer by whom this warrant was executed; do swear that the above inventory contains a true and detailed account of all the property taken by me on the warrant. The attached search warrant was executed on 7/27/01.

1. 5.7 liter Chevrolet Motor serial #
2. 1-five (5) speed transmission serial #

Return made by: _____

Return made to: _____
                     Judge of the District Court
                               Of
                       Canadian County

Figure 3.7. Search warrant return. Provided courtesy of Captain Joe Stanley, El Reno Police Department, El Reno, OK.

ARREST WARRANTS

An affidavit for issuance of an arrest warrant is like a search warrant affidavit. It lays out cause in the first paragraph and then goes on to include personal observations and evidence.

Prepared by the case agent, an affidavit is a synopsis of the entire case presented in one page. In preparing an arrest warrant affidavit, you will review the case notes and summarize them. It is your responsibility to present enough information to convince the judge that there is sufficient evidence to justify issuing an arrest warrant.

You will want to include the parts of the narrative that present compelling evidence and summarize all of the critical information in one page. In your

IN THE DISTRICT COURT IN AND FOR CANADIAN COUNTY

STATE OF OKLAHOMA

THE STATE OF OKLAHOMA,

Plaintiff,

Case No._____

Vs.

James Lewis Blue

Defendant.

AFFIDAVIT FOR ISSUANCE OF ARREST WARRANT
STATE OF OKLAHOMA, COUNTY OF CANADIAN . . . §.

The undersigned, upon oath, deposes and states as follows: to wit: That based on (personal observation) (personal interview of witness) (review of investigative reports) the affiant believes probable cause exists for the issuance of a warrant for the arrest of the defendant named above for the crime(s) of **Knowingly Concealing Stolen Property**. The following testimony and facts received during the investigation indicate the above crime(s) have been committed in Canadian County on or after the 26th Day of April 2001.

I, Lt. Ken W. Brown am a police officer employed by the City of El Reno and am currently assigned to the Detective Division.

> On 7/26/01, Officer Roberts of the El Reno Police Department located a stolen vehicle in the garage located 206 S. Avenue, El Reno. Through the course of the investigation, it was determined the defendant had resided at this residence. Mr. Joe Red reported to Officer Roberts of inquiring about the pickup and the pickup's missing motor from Jason Blue, the brother of the defendant. Jason Blue told Mr. Red that the motor had been taken from the later reported stolen vehicle and placed into his brother's (defendant) white S10 pickup.

> On 7/26/01 your affiant went to 525 S. Street the residence of the defendant where your affiant briefly interviewed the defendant. The defendant stated he had purchased the S10 pickup from Candie Yellow and the motor that was mounted inside of the S10 pickup he purchased from Jason Purple. The defendant further stated Jason Purple had brought the blue 89 Chevrolet Step side pickup to his residence at

Figure 3.8.   Arrest warrant affidavit. Provided courtesy of Captain Joe Stanley, El Reno Police Department, El Reno, OK.

206 S. Avenue sometime during the later part of April 2001. The defendant stated he purchased the pickup for $200.00 however he did not have a title or registration for the Step side pickup.

On 7/27/01 Sgt. Hoehner of the El Reno Police Department received information from Ronald Purple that the motor from the stolen 89Chevrolet Step side pickup had been placed into the defendant's vehicle while at his (Purple) garage located at 1201 S. Avenue, El Reno. Purple further stated the defendant told him the motor was from a vehicle that had been stolen from Edmond Oklahoma. On 8/3/01 your affiant re-interviewed the defendant where he admitted the motor and transmission that were mounted inside of his White Chevrolet S10 had been removed from the stolen 89 Chevrolet Step side pickup. The defendant further admitted to knowing at the time he removed the motor and transmission from the 89 Chevrolet Step side pickup that the vehicle was stolen.

After completing my investigation I feel the above named defendant is in violation of **T 21 § 1713** this being **Knowingly Concealing Stolen Property**.

_____

Affiant, Lt. Ken W. Brown

Figure 3.8.   (*Continued*)

first paragraph, state the specific crime that has been committed and the subject who will be arrested. You will identify yourself as the affiant for the warrant affidavit.

The rest of the affidavit presents the evidence summary in narrative form. The following is an example of an affidavit for issuance of arrest warrant.

SUMMARY

Professional criminal justice writing tasks, such as incident reports, carry special considerations. Officers must always keep in mind that the document may become a matter of public record, and that the document may have many different readers. Narrative reports may be used to determine follow-up activities and whether charges will be filed as a result of the incident.

Report Characteristics

- Correct
- Concise
- Complete

- Clear
- Legible
- Objective

Field Notes

Field notes should be used on the scene to record observations, information, and occurrences. They may serve as resource material for incident reports and any warrants, and may be subpoenaed by other parties.

Narrative Reports

Narrative or incident reports are part of the case record and are often public record. The report will have many different readers and uses, and will require solid writing skills. The incident report is typically made up of three major parts:

The Face Page

The face page is provided by your agency and requests specific information.

The Continuation Page

The continuation page provides a narrative account of information not included on the face page. A good narrative writer will:

- Use chronological order
- Use specific time markers
- Write in past tense
- Write in first person
- Avoid bias

- Use headings
- Avoid repetition
- Proofread carefully
- Take constructive criticism gracefully

Follow-Up Reports

Follow-up reports describe events that take place after the incident. They may be written by a different officer. These materials will become part of the record and are generally narrative.

Supplemental Materials

Supplemental materials may be in a standard form or a narrative, depending on the specifications of your agency. These materials will provide additional information such as evidence reports, search warrants, arrest warrants, case summary statements, photographs, and sketches.

Non-Fatality Traffic Accidents

Non-fatality traffic accidents require little narrative. What narrative you do write will consist of a brief statement summarizing what you observed and witness statements. Diagrams are used in these reports.

Fatality Traffic Accidents

Fatality traffic accidents rely heavily on narrative and supplemental reports. These reports will be used to determine if charges will be filed. Insurance companies may use them to determine liability.

Your report will include your observations, witness statements, photographs, diagrams, supplemental materials, and the medical examiner's report.

Search Warrants

Search warrants involve three components:

> The **Affidavit for Search Warrant** presents the evidence that makes a compelling case to justify the search warrant. The affidavit establishes the credibility of the officer and presents a summary of the investigation.

> The **Search Warrant** is written once probable cause has been established in the Affidavit for Search Warrant. The Search Warrant must specify the place to be searched and the items for which you are searching.

> The **Search Warrant Return** documents who executed the warrant and what items were seized.

Arrest Warrants

The Arrest Warrant is written by the case agent and presents a one-page synopsis of the entire case. The warrant states the specific crime for which the subject will be arrested.

ACTIVITIES

1. Compare the first and second sample narrative reports presented in this chapter. Write an essay in which you address what makes the first report better than the second and how the second report could be improved.

2. Watch a crime scene investigation in a movie or television show. Write a narrative report of the crime.

3. Set up a crime scene for your classmates. Have them write narrative reports and compare the different versions. As a group, select the best report and then revise it.

4. Watch a mystery movie and write a search warrant affidavit and arrest warrant affidavit to create a paper trail for the case.

4

Writing Letters, Reports, and Proposals

JACK OF ALL TRADES

It has been reported that writing occupies 80 percent of an officer's time. This might seem like an unrealistic statistic, but if you stop and think about all of the writing you will do on the job, it adds up quickly.

Consider this: any time you respond to a call, you have to fill out paperwork documenting the nature of the call and what actions were taken. Some cases only require a face page that can be filled out with little or no narrative, while others involve more writing and documentation.

Now consider all of the non-case-related writing you will do on the job. As a member of an agency, you will have to communicate with your colleagues in writing. This involves writing memorandums, email, and short reports. You also might be called upon to communicate with individuals or organizations outside of your agency, and this will involve writing letters and email.

If you go to work for a law enforcement agency and you have good writing skills, there is an excellent chance that you will be called upon to perform writing tasks that benefit your entire agency. These tasks might be in the form of a short report or a grant proposal. If you are comfortable taking on these projects, it can prove helpful to your career.

MEMOS, LETTERS, AND EMAIL

Many circumstances in the workplace can result in the need to write a memorandum, letter, or email to formally communicate with peers, supervisors, or subordinates.

In formal written communication, there are several important factors to consider, such as your purpose, audience, and tone. As with any other form of written communication, memos, letters, and email should be concise, clear, considerate, and professional. All should convey information briefly and accurately, as readers rarely want to wade through a document to find the point. Devices such as bulleted lists and headings can help a busy reader to scan for the important information, so consider using them.

Prewriting Memos and Letters

If the purpose of all written communication is to communicate clearly to every reader, then you, as the writer, need to determine what you are trying to communicate and who your reader will be.

A good question to begin with is, "What do I want to have happen as a result of this document?" This will suggest a starting point for the process. You might also ask yourself, "Why am I writing this document?" By giving yourself a purpose statement, you have essentially given yourself a writing target.

The next question you must answer is about your reader. In internal communication, there are three major groups of readers that you will need to consider: superiors, peers, and subordinates. Your superiors are decision-makers and have knowledge of the broader workings of the institution, but they may be somewhat removed from the field. Keep this in mind when you are writing for this audience. Your peers are professionals at the same level as you within the organization, and subordinates are people who answer to you.

External communication, typically in letter format, is intended for an audience that is outside of your organization. Examples of this type of communication would be letters of recommendation, or letters to school administrators or community leaders about community action programs. With this audience, you will need to try to avoid specialized terminology and jargon.

Writing Memorandums

Memorandums (memos) are used for internal communication. The memo should include an introduction, body, and conclusion. It should also be brief and professional. The format typically includes the following:

To: List the recipients, including titles, one per line

From: Yourself, including title

Subject: Two or three words summarizing the subject of the memo

Date: The date the memo was written

This is one style for memos, but your workplace may have a different format; if this is the case, use the provided format.

Honoring the Chain of Command

There is a wise old saying that goes "Be careful whose toes you step on today; they may be attached to the behind you're kissing tomorrow."

Chain of command is essential to any organization, and violating it can have serious consequences. You should always go through your supervisor when you correspond with anyone at his or her level or above, either by addressing the communication to him or her in addition to the other party, or by including him or her in the copies circulated (cc:) listings. The reason for this is simple: even if you are not intentionally going around your supervisor, he or she should always be informed of the communication you are sending out so he or she does not appear to be uninformed should the topic come up in conversation with his or her superiors.

Writing the Introduction

The introduction should set up the subject of the memo, providing any background information the reader might need to understand the content. If you are writing at someone's request, indicate that you are doing so. If you are writing as the result of an incident, refer to the incident. Although you are writing a brief memo, you want to make sure that the reader understands why the memo is being written and what is being addressed.

Most readers are distracted. The phone rings, people come into the office, other tasks require attention. Your memo should clearly indicate how the topic relates to him or her and why reading it deserves their time.

If you are writing a memo about attending a training session, your introduction might read:

> I am writing in response to the memo you sent about the report-writing training which will be offered on August 17, 2003. I am interested in attending this training session.

This introduction clearly indicates the purpose for the memo, what it is in response to, and what action is desired.

Writing the Body

Now that you have established the purpose of the memo for the reader, you will want to develop the body by offering more specific details. Anticipate what information the reader will need in order to decide what action to take as a result of this memo. In the example given in the introduction, the memo recipient will need additional information. Why do you need the training? How will you benefit? How will the department benefit? Who will cover your work assignment while you attend this training (if you have input in this decision).

Remember that readers rarely read an entire document, preferring to pick out the important information, so make this information easily accessible. If the material lends itself, you might want to use bullets or headings to direct the reader's attention to important sections.

Writing the Conclusion

The last things that you will want to do in your memo are summarize the content, restate the desired outcome, and offer the reader a follow-up action. Following this format offers the reader a recap of the important information and clearly indicates what needs to be done next.

Keeping the Tone Professional

The tone of your memo should always be courteous and professional. If you are writing about an emotionally charged subject, make sure to maintain a respectful tone. Appearing to be antagonistic or sarcastic will only undermine your argument

Interoffice Memo

Date: 6/7/2002
To: Captain Sam Smith
From: Sgt. Joe Friday

RE: Training Seminar on Writing

I am writing in response to the memo you sent about the report-writing training, which will be offered on August 17, 2003. I am interested in attending this training session.

As you may recall, my last performance evaluation indicated that writing police reports is an area I need to work on. Being allowed to attend this training session will enable me to improve my writing skills so that I will not have to revise my narrative reports before they are submitted into the evidence file. I have spoken to several officers who have attended this training, and they all said that the information presented was very helpful. As you know, I am always interested in improving my skills.

Please consider selecting me to attend this writing training seminar. If you have any questions, please contact me.

Figure 4.1.   Sample memo

and alienate your reader. Never appear to be accusing or defensive—this will only weaken your credibility.

Should the circumstance arise when you find yourself writing a potentially volatile memo, make sure to give yourself time to calm down before writing and sending it. You might also have a colleague read the memo to make sure that the tone is professional and free of language that might carry negative connotations. If at all possible, write the memo and let it rest for a day before sending it, leaving time for one final revision.

Writing Letters

Unlike memos, letters are usually written to individuals or groups outside of the agency. If you are writing in an official capacity as a spokesperson for your organization, you will want to use letterhead stationery. Don't underestimate the responsibility that comes with the use of this letterhead; as a spokesperson for your organization, it is particularly important that you use excellent writing skills. Remember that your entire organization might be judged by the quality of your correspondence, so proofread very carefully.

As with writing memos, you will want to include an introduction, body, and conclusion.

Writing the Introduction

In a letter, you will need to include more introductory information, as your reader will probably not be aware of the reasons behind the communication. For example, if you were writing a letter to area schools about the introduction of a school violence prevention program, you would probably want to begin by explaining what the program is, why there is a need for the program, and how it will affect the schools.

As with any document, readers are busy and they will be inclined to discard your letter unless they understand why it applies to them. You will need to "hook" your reader in the introduction. In the example of the school violence prevention program, you might want to start out with a startling statistic about the rate of school violence or a quote from an expert on the topic. From there, you will want to introduce yourself, your program (briefly), and tell the reader what you are offering.

Writing the Body

Now that you have your reader's attention, you need to give specific details. Make sure to answer any questions that the reader might have about your subject. Remember that your reader might not be informed about the topic, so include enough supporting material to thoroughly explain the concept. Avoid using jargon or specialized language; your reader is not a law enforcement professional, in all likelihood. If you are writing about starting a school violence

June 8, 2002

Dr. Leslie Smith,
Superintendent of Schools
400 S. Education Boulevard
Anytown, Anystate 00123

Dear Dr. Smith:

Research shows that students feel increasingly unsafe during school, or traveling to and from school. A 1996 Children's Institute International Poll of American Adolescents revealed that 47 percent of all teens believed their schools were becoming more violent, 10 percent feared being shot or hurt by classmates carrying weapons to schools, and more than 20 percent were afraid to go to restrooms because these unsupervised areas were frequent sites of student victimization.

(National Center for Educational Statistics, 1998)

As a member of the Anytown Police Department, I am concerned about the national increase in school violence. Rather than wait for an incident to occur in our community, the Anytown Police Department is reaching out to establish a school violence prevention program partnership between our police department and our schools. This program will allow students to gain access to education without fear.

The Anytown School Violence Prevention Program will involve a cooperative agreement between the public schools, the police department, and Anytown Youth and Family Services. The Anytown Police Department is requesting a $100,000 implementation grant from the Department of Justice to establish and administer this program. The project has three major stakeholders.

The Police Department

The Anytown police department will provide:

- School violence prevention training sessions for school employees
- A School Resource Officer assigned to the schools to serve as a law enforcement officer and as a prevention training teacher
- School violence prevention assemblies and workshops for students
- Funding for all elements of the prevention program

Figure 4.2.   Sample letter

Youth and Family Services

Through the partnership, Youth and Family Services will provide:

- Individual and/or family counseling for students who display violent behavior
- Individual and/or family counseling for students who have been victims of school violence
- Workshops for school counselors
- Research materials related to violence prevention

Anytown Public Schools

As a partner in this program, your school will be asked to provide the following services:

- Form a parent advisory board for the violence prevention program
- Form a student advisory committee for the violence prevention program
- Encourage students to form a chapter of S.A.V.E. (Students Against Violence Everywhere)
- Allow employees to attend training sessions (the grant will provide funding for substitute teachers)
- Schedule time for student assemblies
- Work with the partner stakeholders to ensure the success of the program

As members of a society that has seen an alarming increase in youth violence, the Anytown Police Department is eager to submit this grant proposal, but first we must obtain letters of agreement from all of the stakeholders.

I would like to schedule a meeting so that we can discuss more of the specific details about this proposal, and so that I can seek further input from you. Please call me at 555-5555 as soon as possible to schedule a meeting. I am available Monday through Friday between 8:00 and 5:00. I am looking forward to working with you on this project.

Sincerely,

Officer Laura Rogers

Figure 4.2.   (*Continued*)

prevention program, you might want to write a paragraph about the history and make up of the program. Another paragraph might be devoted to explaining the details of the program, and a third paragraph might explain how the school can participate in the program.

Writing the Conclusion

Once you have presented all of the important information, you will want to conclude with a brief summary and a call to action. Recap the important details, and then offer your reader the next step, such as contacting you. Be sure to include your contact information and what times you are available for follow-up. You might also offer to set up a meeting at the reader's convenience, if that is appropriate in the situation. End on an up-note. Let your reader know that you are looking forward to hearing from him or her.

Writing Electronic Mail

With Internet service so readily available, many agencies rely on electronic mail (email) for in-house communication. This technology has streamlined communication in the workplace and at home, but the convenience also has a cost. As a writer, you should always keep in mind your audience and task, even when you are using email. There are a few basic writing and communication skills that you should keep in mind when you are using email.

Check Email Often

Not checking your email regularly defeats the entire purpose of the technology. The benefit of email is that delivery is nearly instantaneous, so your readers expect that you will read your email often. This doesn't mean that you have to obsess over email and check it every fifteen minutes, but it is a good idea to check your email in the morning and in the afternoon. Read the communications you have received and see what response you might need to make.

Respond Promptly

Don't put off responding to emails. Again, because the delivery method is immediate, correspondents expect timely responses. Give yourself enough time to provide an appropriate response, but don't put off answering emails indefinitely. Many email systems have built-in message tracking enabling senders to know exactly when you read the message, so resist the temptation to buy time by saying that you haven't received the email.

Sometimes the information requested in an email may be so detailed that it is better to respond in person. If this is the case, you should send a response indicating that you will meet with the sender. After the meeting, you might want to send a follow-up email summarizing the details.

Respond Professionally

Follow all the rules of written communication when you compose an email. You should pay attention to spelling and grammar, organize well, and keep a professional tone. Always be aware that your email can be forwarded to others, so be careful what you write.

You should also be aware that you have no right to privacy on an email account provided by your employer, so do not send or receive personal emails at work that you would not want your employer to read. As with any written communication, email provides a paper trail that can work for you or against you, so use good judgment.

Avoid the Pitfalls of Email

Occasionally you might receive an email that just rubs you the wrong way, so to speak. In these cases, it is tempting to respond aggressively, sarcastically, or defensively, and worse, to do so immediately. None of these response methods will be productive, so resist!

The best course of action in this situation is to allow a cooling-off period. If you just can't walk away, then go ahead and let it rip—but not in an email. Write a response using a word processing program. Get all of those pent-up feelings out on paper. Then walk away from what you have written. Reread the response after some time has passed and then rewrite it so that the tone is professional. You might also have a trusted colleague read the letter and give you feedback.

Another temptation of email is to send blind copies (bcc) or to forward emails you have received without the permission or knowledge of the sender. These actions are considered discourteous.

Always remember that professionalism is the key to email in the workplace. Allow yourself time to compose an appropriate and thoughtful response to any message, and be courteous and considerate.

WRITING SHORT REPORTS

If you are called upon to write a short report, you have a choice to make. If the report is for interdepartmental use, you should use a memo format. Unless you are an administrator reporting to the city council or the mayor, this is the most common type of short report writing you will do. If the report is to an outside party, use a cover letter and report format.

As with any other communication, remember that your reader will probably be distracted by daily interruptions. Make the message clear. Use the introduction, body, and conclusion format, and include a recommendation in the conclusion. You will also want to use headings to separate the sections of the report so that your reader can choose which sections are relevant to his or her needs.

In the introduction, include a clear overview of the problem or issue you will be addressing. Support the introduction with specific evidence in the body of the report. Use statistics and incidents to illustrate the issue for the reader. Make sure to include enough information for your reader to make an educated decision. Finally, in your conclusion, summarize the contents of the report and make recommendations.

Remember that short reports are just that: short. Don't pad it—readers have other things to do and will not wade through a long document.

The following is an example of a short report:

EL RENO POLICE DEPARTMENT

MEMO

TO: Capt. Savage

FROM: Lt. Brown

DATE: September 30, 2000

SUBJ: Excessive False Alarms

As you may or may not be aware we receive a horrendous amount of false alarms to the same businesses as well as some private residences. Back in April of 1999, the City adopted ordinance # 120 (1-8). This ordinance lays out definitions, guidelines and procedures for notification and enforcement action for excessive false alarms.

The practice has been to basically ignore the problem and Officers are responding to the same alarm(s) over and over again without the business owner(s) taking any measure to resolve the problem and in many cases not respond to the alarm unless there is a problem. The ordinance calls for a night number or key holder to respond to the activated alarm and failure to do so results in the alarm being counted as a false alarm.

Figure 4.3.   Sample short report. Printed by permission of Ken W. Brown, El Reno Police Department, El Reno, OK.

The ordinance also requires the communication director give written notice of the false alarm to the Police or Fire Chief and after review send notice to the owner, resident or occupant from which the false alarm originates. Three false alarms within 90 days by ordinance are deemed excessive and the owner or resident can be cited with the maximum fine of $200.00. In an effort to resolve this problem, I am requesting that we start enforcing this ordinance with notification to the business owner of the false alarm and maintain an alarm log so citations can be issued for enforcement. I have instructed my personnel to require a night number or key holder to respond to the activated alarm if available.

I would recommend as an option for documentation that we issue warning notice to the responding night number or key holder and maintain these warning citation in file for court room testimony. I have attached a copy of the ordinance and a recommendation for handling the false alarm calls for your review.

Procedure for handling false alarms

1. Respond as normal and determine alarm status.
2. If owner/resident/occupant is not on location require night number or key holder to respond.
3. If the alarm is determined to be false, verify with communication division the number of false alarms responded to within past 90 days.
4. If less than 3, issue a written warning.
5. Turn the written warning over to the communication division for entry on the alarm log and then foreword to the communication director. The warning would then be filed for courtroom presentation if needed.
6. The communication director or his designee would send notice of the false alarm and the number of false alarms received with the past 90 days to the business or resident owner with notice of possible penalties.
7. If the fourth false alarm occurs within the 90-day period, citation to be issued to the business or resident owner.

I would also recommend each business be contacted either personally or by mail informing/reminding them of the ordinance and the procedure be followed, and that a news release be placed in the local paper notifying the residence owners of the ordinance and procedure. This would also be a great time to get up to date information for night numbers or additional key holders.

Figure 4.3. (*Continued*)

WRITING PROPOSALS

Because law enforcement agencies are publicly funded, there is always a need for more money to purchase equipment, develop programs, and hire personnel. Government agencies such as the Department of Justice send out notices of grant opportunities for specific purposes. Browsing these grant announcements will help you to see what types of programs are being funded so that you will know what opportunities exist and which may apply to your agency.

Finding Grant Opportunities

One excellent Internet resource for finding grants is Law Enforcement Grants Resources On The Internet (http://www.viperpolice.com/grants/). This site offers links to funding opportunities, including those of the Community Oriented Policing Services (Department of Justice), The National Institute of Justice, the United States Department of Justice, Bureau of Justice Assistance, Office of Juvenile Justice and Delinquency Prevention, Violence Against Women Office (Department of Justice), Drug Courts Program Office (Department of Justice), Corrections Program Office (Department of Justice), Office for Victims of Crime (Department of Corrections), and Universal Hiring Program (COPS, Department of Justice).

When you access these links, you will generally find the program history and description, current funding opportunities, and a grant writer's toolkit. These resources are invaluable for a grant writer. Read all of the information presented by the granting agency and access the tips for grant writers. You might also want to attend the grant writing workshops that are offered regionally across the United States.

Above all else, when you locate a grant that you want to pursue, download the format and the forms that are provided in the toolkit. Failing to follow the prescribed formula or submit the required forms can cost you the funding opportunity.

Requests for Proposals (RFPs) are updated continually, and there are often multiple cycles for the same grant, so if you miss one deadline, go for the next. If you find a grant that you want to pursue and the closing date is too close to meet, look for the next cycle and start preparing your information. It is a good idea to record upcoming deadlines on your calendar so you won't forget. Additionally, some grants have a two-stage application process. The first stage is simply a letter of intent that indicates that your agency will be applying for a grant. This letter helps the funding agency anticipate how many grant proposals will need to be evaluated.

Understanding the Grant Process

Once a granting agency receives its funding initiatives for the fiscal year, it allocates funding priorities, sets up the grant cycles, prepares the grant materials, and sends out RFPs and application deadlines.

Make contact with your regional agency grant coordinator. This person is available to help you with the technical aspects of writing your grant. The granting agency will also publish any grant writing training sessions that are being offered. Try to attend one of these training sessions.

The granting agency will also have a list of funded grants from the previous grant cycle. It is helpful to get a copy of a successful proposal to use as a model. You can get a copy of a funded proposal from the granting agency or from the agency that wrote the proposal.

Once the granting agency has received your letter of intent or proposal, it will send out a call for grant evaluators. Professionals from related areas will be selected and trained in grant evaluation. Once the evaluators are trained, they will be divided into review panels and given a set of proposals to evaluate, along with review criteria and response forms.

The reviewers will read the proposals and evaluate them, and then the panels will meet to discuss the proposals and to compare their evaluations of each proposal. Specifically, the reviewers will be looking for strengths and weaknesses in each section so they can assign a score. Scores are assigned to each section and then they will be tallied for an overall score.

Grants are awarded to the proposals that score the most points, so you will want to make sure to anticipate and correct any weaknesses before you submit your grant proposal.

Grant reviewers are given a very short time-frame for completing the review process. To make your proposal effective, be sure to follow all of the instructions for the proposal, use the prescribed headings, include information in tables (in addition to the narrative) for quick reference, and keep your writing concise. Reviewers do not have time to search for information that is not included in the proper section, so make it easy for them.

In many cases, reviewers are given five or fewer days to review ten or more proposals, and they are cloistered in a hotel away from home. By following the format exactly, providing thorough and concise explanations, and addressing every element of the grant, you will make their jobs easier.

Once the reviewers have finished evaluating and scoring, the proposals and scoring and comment sheets are turned in to the grant competition administrator. The scores are then rated, and the notification process begins.

After the grants have been awarded, the successful applicants will usually be required to attend a grant negotiation meeting. At this meeting, the grantor and the grant administrator from the requesting agency will discuss modifications and specifications for the grant. Some budget items may be altered, for example, or the grantor might ask for program modifications. After the terms are agreed upon, a contract will be issued.

Federal grants are closely monitored, so you will be expected to submit progress reports to the grantor about status, expenses, and outcomes. You should expect to have grant monitors visit your site at some point in the grant cycle, and you will be expected to submit an end-of-grant report.

Writing the Grant

Writing a successful grant requires time, research, and patience. A poorly re-searched grant has a very slim chance of making it past peer reviewers, as they are trained to look for weaknesses and they are familiar with law enforcement. You will need to have access to statistics, records, budgets, and histories. You will also need to have some idea of what other agencies in your area and state are doing that might relate to your proposal.

You will also need to have the support of your department and community. Many grants call for letters of support and assurance of participation from stake-holders, so be sure to allow time and planning for these resources. You also need to remember that grant writing is a team project. You cannot be expected to have all of the information required to write the grant, so be sure to identify key people who can help you with the task.

Typically, a proposal will have the following sections:

- Statement of the problem
- Goals and objectives
- Project strategy or design
- Implementation timeline
- Proposed budget
- Budget narrative

- Matching commitments
- Program evaluation
- Management structure and organizational capability
- Civil rights assurance

This chapter offers a general overview of what information might be included in each section, but always follow the guidelines of the granting agency. The guide-lines for specific grants will list the sections and offer explanations of what infor-mation should be included.

Read the grant writing guidelines very carefully. Some RFPs give very spe-cific guidelines for the proposal. For example, some guidelines specify paper size and orientation, font (type) size, and section lengths, and number of copies to be submitted. You will also want to make sure that you have all of the required forms filled out and signed by the appropriate people.

Statement of the Problem

This is the first section of the grant. You will need to be as persuasive as possible in this section because it establishes the level of need your agency has for the grant. This section will provide a clear and concise picture of the nature and scope of the problem that will be addressed by the funding sought from the grantor. In this section you will address:

The nature, scope, and history of the problem, as well as how it affects the jurisdictional area

Statistics and other information related to the area addressed by the proposal, including an analysis of the statistics

An explanation of the history of the problem, including what actions have been taken to address it in the past

A description of how the statistics and other information were used to assess the problem

Remember that this is the first section the reviewers will read, and this section usually carries a high number of points. Research this section thoroughly and present information that proves to the reviewers that there is a significant problem that meets the criteria of the grant. You want to convince your reviewers that the need is sufficient to justify awarding the grant to you.

Goals and Objectives

This section will outline the goals for your grant. The goals and objectives must be specific and measurable, as they will serve as the measure of the success of your project.

Goals Goals are broad statements that address how the project will meet the need established in the grant. A goal for a school violence prevention program might be: "To reduce the number of incidents of school violence in Anywhere Public Schools."

Make sure that your goal statements are directly related to the need and to the problem addressed by the grant.

Objectives Program objectives are specific and measurable statements that reflect the specific steps that will be taken to meet the stated goal. Each goal should have its own set of specific objectives. Objectives to meet the goal of reducing the number of incidents of school violence in Anywhere Public Schools might be:

Offer three school assemblies addressing conflict resolution
Install metal detectors at all school entrances
Hire three additional security personnel to monitor hallways and restrooms
Offer two employee violence prevention training sessions

Remember that you are setting your own measurement standards, and your program will be evaluated by these standards, but you also need to set measurable standards using specific numbers and percentages.

Project Strategy or Design

The project strategy or design will provide a detailed narrative of how the project will be implemented. In this narrative, you will need to offer a detailed explanation of how the program will be implemented and operated by your agency. You will need to include:

- Innovative strategies and designs for the implementation of the project
- Specific services that will be provided by the project
- A detailed description of who will benefit from the project
- Project stakeholders, including partners and other participants
- A description of how this project will function within the existing structure of your agency and that of other stakeholders
- An explanation of how the outcomes of your project will be disseminated to others so that it might serve a larger community
- An explanation of what innovations will be offered by this project
- A detailed explanation of why you think this project will successfully address the problem

Table 4.1. Sample implementation timeline

MILESTONE	COMPLETION DATE	PERSON RESPONSIBLE	STAKEHOLDERS AFFECTED
Form program taskforce	July 2004	Grant Director	Police department Youth and family services Public schools
Place school safety officer	August 2004	Grant Director	Public schools Students
Conduct training for teachers	August 2004	Grant Director	Public school employees Youth and family services
Form parent advisory committee	September 2004	Public School Coordinator	Public school employees Parents
Form student advisory committee	September 2004	Public School Coordinator	Students
Conduct first violence prevention assembly	September 2004	Youth and Family Services	Public schools Students
Form chapter of S.A.V.E.	October 2004	Student Advisory Committee	Students

Implementation Timeline

The timeline should be addressed in table form, as shown in Table 4.1. You should align each of your implementation stages as a milestone and provide a target date for the completion of each milestone. Additionally, you might list key personnel who are responsible for the completion of each milestone and what key personnel or stakeholders will assist. Break the table down into the distinct steps that will be taken to meet the program outcomes and make sure to set realistic deadlines. You might also consider including the goals and objectives that will be met or affected by each milestone.

Proposed Budget

The budget is a key element of your proposal. You need to do thorough research to determine the cost of each element of the project, and you must justify all of the expenses.

In most cases, the grantor will provide a budget worksheet and budget form. Typically, the budget is broken down into several different categories. The grant format will specify the categories, but typically they are divided into the following:

> **Personnel** List each position by title and name of employee, if available. The grant should only pay for the percentage of that person's time that will be devoted to the grant. For example, if an employee will spend 25 percent of his or her time (10 hours per week for a 40-hour per week employee), then you will allocate 25 percent of his or her salary to the grant. Most grants also specify that grant-funded employees must be paid at the same scale as non-grant employees involved in similar work, so be sure to be consistent.

> **Fringe Benefits** Fringe benefits should be based on actual known costs or on an established formula. Your personnel officer should be able to tell you what percentage of pay is calculated for this category. Calculate the benefits for each employee paid by the grant using the same percentage as you used to determine the salary. If you are paying 25 percent of an employee's salary from grant funds, then pay 25 percent of the fringe benefits from the grant.

> **Travel** Travel expenses should be separated and itemized. Specify the purpose of the travel and make sure it is related to the grant project. You also need to show how the figure was calculated and break it down per person. You can usually break down travel by separating budget items into mileage, airfare, lodging, and food. Make sure to familiarize yourself with per diem and other spending limitations of the granting agency.

Equipment Provide an itemized list of the equipment that will be needed for the grant as well as the cost. Include such items as computers, photo-copiers, fax machines, scanners, and furniture. Limit this category to non-expendable items. Each item cost should be researched to make sure you have requested a reasonable amount.

Supplies Itemize the expendable supplies that will be used for your project. These might include paper, staples, paper clips, photocopying, postage, books, and computer disks.

Consultants/Contracts If you will be hiring consultants, specify the nature of the training, the identity of the consultant, and the cost per day. Research any caps the grantor may have placed on daily consulting fees and do not exceed them without justification. You should also itemize other related consultant expenses such as travel, lodging, and meals. Follow the same guidelines for any other contractual employees you may hire and make sure to relate them to the grant. For example, if you are purchasing a computer and linking it to a network, you might have to contract with a networking specialist.

Other Costs Include an itemized list and the computational method used to arrive at estimates for such items as office space rental, utilities, phone lines, etc.

Budget Narrative

Once you have completed the budget worksheet and form, you might want to include a budget narrative that offers further explanation of each budget item and how it relates to the project. Although this may not be necessary, it offers you another opportunity to persuade the reviewers that your costs are reasonable. If you choose to write a budget narrative, include a heading that matches the category heading on the budget sheet and write a brief paragraph offering justification for the items.

Matching Commitments

Some grants require matching funds while others do not. In either case, procuring matching funds and services indicates that your agency has a commitment to supporting this project. Funding from other sources, such as another grant or funding from a city, will strengthen your proposal. The matching funds do not have to be monetary: if a school is offering you free office space or secretarial support, attach a dollar value to these services and include them in this category. Make sure to indicate how you arrived at the calculation and who will be providing the service or funding.

Program Evaluation

The success of a grant must be measurable, so you will need to set up evaluation methods. Provide measurements for implementation as well as overall project evaluation. You also need to include a detailed explanation of what data will be used for program assessment and how the data will be gathered and analyzed. Tie your measurement back to your goals and objectives.

You should also indicate how your evaluation information will be used. For example, you might use the evaluation results to make program modifications to improve the project in the future.

Management Structure and Organizational Capability

The management structure section addresses the organizational structure of the agency and partners, and how the grant personnel and structure will fit into the current organizational structure. You might include an organizational chart and narrative to support this section.

You will also want to offer a subsection about key personnel on the grant, including their positions and qualifications. Be sure to include a clear chain of command that is linked to your department.

Civil Rights Assurance

If you are applying for federal grant funding, you will be required to include a civil rights assurance statement. Your agency will have an Equal Employment Opportunity statement, so include this. You might also include a statement assuring that you will make an effort to recruit minority and under-represented groups for this project.

Attaching Required Forms

In your application tool kit, you will find the forms that are required for the grant. Follow the directions for completing the forms, obtain the required signatures, and attach the forms in the specified order. Most grant tool kits provide a checklist and downloadable forms. Make sure that you have completed all of the required forms before you mail your proposal.

Make sure that you send the required number of copies of the proposal, and keep at least one complete copy for your own reference.

2002 EDWARD BYRNE MEMORIAL FORMULA GRANT PROGRAM
Application Form

1. **Purpose Area of the Project:** Multi-Jurisdictional Task Force Program

2. **Project Title:** Canadian County Drug Task Force (CCDTF)

3. **Agency Applicant:** El Reno Police Department

4. **Applicant Mailing Address:** 116 N. Evans, El Reno Oklahoma 73036

   Area Code/Phone Number: 405-262-6941

   Area Code/Fax Number: 405-262-2128

5. **Project Director:** Capt. Fred Savage

6. **Project Director Contact Information:**

   Address: 116 N. Evans

   City: El Reno

   State/Zip: Oklahoma, 73036

   Phone Number: 405-262-6941

   Fax Number: 405-262-2128

7. **Fiscal Officer:** Orvel Gibson

8. **Fiscal Officer Contact Information:**

   Address: Post Office Box 700

   City: El Reno

   State/Zip: Oklahoma 73036

   Phone Number: 405-262-4070 ext. 225

   Fax Number: 405-262-9618

9. **Federal Tax Identification Number:** 73-6005-196

10. **Congressional District Covered:** Five (5) and Six (6)

Figure 4.4. Sample grant proposal. Printed by permission of Ken W. Brown, El Reno Police Department, El Reno, OK.

11. Project Land Area: 896.4 Square Miles

12. Population Served: 87,041

13. Federal Amount Requested: _____
Cash Match: (Divide the federal request by 3)   _____
Total Project Cost: (Fed Amount + Cash Match)   _____

14. Previous Funding for This Project:

Grant Year: 1998 (D98-846)   Amount: $ 70,000.00 (Federal Amount)
Grant Year: 1999 (D99-098)   Amount: $ 50,000.00 (Federal Amount)
Grant Year: 2000 (D00-1021)   Amount: $ 72,812.00 (Federal Amount)
Grant Year: 2001 (D01-1071)   Amount: $ 85,000.00 (Federal Amount)

15. If awarded, these funds will: (check all that apply)

_____ Create a new service or activity

_____ Enhance an existing project

____✓_____ Continuation of a current federally funded project

16. List Source(s) of Match for this Project:
Project Income, Salary Benefits

17. Compliance with Fiscal and Programmatic Reporting Requirements: (mark one)

            Compliance has been met for all fiscal and programmatic reporting requirements
__✓____ of previously awarded grants from the District Attorney's Council.

            Compliance has **not** been met for all fiscal and programmatic reporting
_____ requirements of previously awarded grants from the District Attorney's Council.

Figure 4.4.   (*Continued*)

MULTI-JURISDICTIONAL DRUG TASK FORCES ONLY – PROJECT INCOME
Multi-Jurisdictional Drug Task Forces are required to report all court-awarded project income on a quarterly basis throughout the funding period. List all project income for the Grant Year 00, which ended June 30, 2001, and the amount of project income that was shared with other law enforcement agencies.

Grant Year 00	Amount of Project Income	Amount of Project Income Shared with other Law Enforcement Entities
First Quarter	$ 0	$
Second Quarter	$ 0	$
Third Quarter	$ 4802.14	$ 3620.81
Fourth Quarter	$	$
TOTAL	$ 4802.14	$ 3620.81

18. MULTI-JURISDICTIONAL DRUG TASK FORCES ONLY – INTERAGENCY COLLABORTION
List all of the agencies and jurisdictions with which there is collaboration.

Canadian County Sheriff's Office _____   _____

Mustang Police Department _____   _____

Piedmont Police Department _____   _____

Okarche Police Department _____   _____

Calumet Police Department _____   _____

Canadian County District Attorney's Office _____   _____

Union City Police Department _____   _____

_____   _____

_____   _____

_____   _____

_____   _____

Figure 4.4.   (*Continued*)

**20. CRIMINAL HISTORY INFORMATION SYSTEMS/PROSECUTION
    MANAGEMENT SYSTEM PROGRAMS ONLY**

Complete the information below as required for this purpose area.

    a. Is the applicant agency aware of the Oklahoma Plan for Criminal History Records
       improvement?   Yes   No

    b. Is the applicant agency in compliance with Title 74, Section 150.10-150.12?
                       Yes   No

    c. Is the applicant agency in compliance with FBI and NIST requirements?
                       Yes   No

    d. Explain how this application is related to the above referenced Plan.

Figure 4.4. *(Continued)*

APPLICATION NARRATIVE
PROBLEM STATEMENT AND PROJECT DESCRIPTION

In approximately 1995, the El Reno Police Department experienced an eruption in drug activity in the community, along with the associated violence with several shootings and drug related homicides. The department established a special investigations unit made up of two patrol officers who primarily engaged in drug investigations on their off duty time. The formation of the unit was necessary due to the lack of any organized narcotic investigation since the disbandment of the previous Drug Task Force in approximately 1990. The Canadian County Sheriff's Department as well as the surrounding law enforcement agencies of Canadian County also lacked the ability due to manpower and financial resources to devote personnel to narcotic enforcement on a full time basis.

With the success of the special investigations unit and the obvious shortcomings of such a unit, the El Reno Police Department pursued funding for a fully-funded Narcotic Investigation Unit. In 1998, we received funding from your committee for the establishment of a full time drug unit, which has seen significant success.

During the first year (1998), the unit worked with the Drug Enforcement Administration's Mobile Enforcement Team (MET), which marked their first Oklahoma deployment. Our attempt to obtain their assistance took approximately one year, and they arrived shortly after we began with our drug unit. Through the investigation, over twenty-three people were arrested and charged for a variety of drug distribution charges, the majority of which were prosecuted in federal court. Not only were several local crack cocaine dealers arrested, a drug source in Houston was identified and arrested, along with two Colombians, all of which impacted not only our city but the entire state.

During the second year (1999) of operation, the focus of the unit shifted to methamphetamine distribution and manufacturing. With the increased enforcement in the metropolitan areas and the ease in which methamphetamine is manufactured; the El Reno area experienced a sudden increase in the number of clandestine methamphetamine laboratories. Based on the 2000 data from the Oklahoma State Bureau of Investigation as well as local data, Canadian County ranked first in Western Oklahoma and in the top twelve counties of Oklahoma for clandestine laboratory seizures with a total of seventeen (17).

During the third year (2000) a third investigator was added to the Drug Task Force provided by the Canadian County Sheriff's Department, we were able to expand into a truly county wide drug task force. The focus of the grant remained on methamphetamine distribution and manufacturing and expanded to the distribution of precursors for manufacturing of methamphetamine and distribution as well as the distribution of marijuana and crack cocaine not only in El Reno but throughout Canadian County and the adjoining counties.

In the fourth year of operation (2001) the Drug Task Force has focus on identifying higher-level suppliers and distributors of methamphetamine and those responsible for the cooking of methamphetamine. The Task Force teams has identified the top ten in our area and from the top ten have arrested and prosecuted three to date. The team has seen an increase in the number of active and box methamphetamine labs (19 year to date). During the current grant year, we have added two additional clandestine lab certified personnel to the Methamphetamine Laboratory Response Team.

Figure 4.4. (*Continued*)

In addition to the cases presented at the Federal Court Level, the team has been responsible for and/or assisted in cases, which have been filed in Kingfisher County, Caddo County, Blaine County as well as Caddo and Canadian County District Court.

The team has participated in investigations with Mustang Police Department, Calumet Police Department, Piedmont Police Department, Hinton Police Department, Union City Police Department, Blaine County Sheriff's Office, District 6 Drug Task Force, Oklahoma Highway Patrol (Troop A), Oklahoma Bureau of Narcotic's, Drug Enforcement Administration and the Federal Bureau of Prisons (El Reno). Additionally over the last three years, the El Reno Police Department, Yukon Police Department and the Canadian County Sheriff's Department had instituted drug interdiction programs working Interstate 40 and State Hwy 81.

During the 2000 grant year, the Canadian County Drug Task Force came into a written agreement with the Canadian County District Attorneys Office for a percentage of the funds collected from seizures (a first for any law enforcement agency within Canadian County). We have obtained the needed equipment and have developed a Methamphetamine Laboratory Response Team to aid area Law Enforcement agencies in detection, safe response and prosecution of clandestine methamphetamine laboratories. We have joined with local businesses and citizens to recognize suspected clandestine laboratory operations and with the help of local media along with the web site developed by the El Reno Police Department, we are seeing results from information provided by citizens and businesses responding to the news articles.

The El Reno Police Department was able to obtain a drug detection dog through private donations and funds obtained through the District Attorneys Revolving Drug Fund and have committed personnel to assist the task force on investigations on an "as needed" basis. This is in addition to the Canadian County Sheriff's Department's K-9 Unit which has committed the use of their canines and handlers. We have also joined the Canadian County Special Response team to provide needed resources in serving search warrants on suspected drug operations.

The El Reno Police Department has pledged to administer the grant and to provide two personnel funded through the proposed grant. The Canadian County Sheriff's Office has pledged one person to be devoted to the task force funded through the proposed grant and other law enforcement agencies in the county have pledged support in the form of either monetary, personnel or assistance when needed. The task force will continue in the effort to reduce the amount of illegal drugs by the continuation of a larger multi-agency drug task force. If funded, the task force plans to continue to target distributors of illegal drugs, target clandestine methamphetamine operations, enhance the clandestine methamphetamine response team, assist drug interdiction personnel in dissemination of drug intelligence, case preparation and follow-up along with enhancing public awareness of illegal drugs particularly clandestine methamphetamine laboratory recognition. This will be accomplished by using all media resources available, the El Reno Police Department/Canadian County Drug Task Force Web Site and through other personnel assigned to assist the task force in completing this goal.

The task force will continue to have inter-local agreement between the various law enforcement agencies. The task force will continue to hold regular meetings in which intelligence can be exchanged, investigative targets identified and case status be discussed. Task Force personnel will be

Figure 4.4. (*Continued*)

responsible for regular reporting to the District Attorney's Council as required by the grant. Utilizing personnel from the project, drug offenders may be interviewed for case prosecution, intelligence and cultivation of confidential informants. Task Force personnel will continue relationships with other jurisdictions to expand drug investigations as needed. Task Force Personnel will also serve as a point of contact with other law enforcement agencies to facilitate intelligence and investigations as related to illegal drugs and other criminal acts. The task force will continue to aid other law enforcement agencies in the detection, safe response and prosecution of clan meth labs. Law Enforcement and Public education will also be enhanced for businesses and citizens to recognize suspected clan lab operations with the assistance of other personnel from within the police department.

APPLICATION NARRATIVE
GOALS, OBJECTIVES, PERFORMANCE MEASURES AND ACTIVITIES

- The goals, objectives, performance measures and activities of a grant proposal are inherently related
- **Goals** are broad, general statements of a desired result or outcome of the project.
- **Objectives** are specific results or effects of a program's activities that must be achieved to reach the goals. Objectives must include performance measures that are specific and measurable. The performance measures identify quantifiable data that determine whether the goals and objectives are met.
- **Activities** are the specific steps taken to meet the objectives.
- Use the following outline format in this sections:
    1. Goals
        A. Objectives/Performance Measures
            1. Activities
- See Appendix A for further information on how to write goals, objectives/performance measures and activities.
- Do not delete these directions. If more space is necessary use additional pages.

1. (*Goal*) – Increase membership in the Methamphetamine Laboratory Response Team and equipment required to investigate Clandestine Labs within Canadian County.

> (*Objective*) – To increase team by two members. (***Performance Indicator*** Number of Clandestine Lab Certified Investigators assigned to the Task Force).

   A.

   1. (*Activity*) – Solicit agreements with agency administrators through phone calls and individual meetings.
   2. (*Activity*) – Solicit members from agencies within Task Force Jurisdiction
   3. (*Activity*) – Purchase one additional SCBA equipment through funds received by grant award.
   4. (*Activity*) – Enrollment of two additional officers in Clandestine Lab training held by either OSBI or DEA during grant year.

Figure 4.4.   (*Continued*)

B. *(Objective)* – Supply minimum of two Clandestine Lab certified Investigators upon request of any agency within Canadian County. (**Performance Indicator** Rotation schedule available upon request, Number of meth labs seized)

    1. *(Activity)* – Develop monthly rotating call-out list with necessary contact names and numbers.

    2. *(Activity)* – Supply all agencies within Canadian County a monthly on-call investigators list for Clan Lab investigations.

2. *(Goal)* – Provide training to Law Enforcement officers in the recognition, seizure, dismantling and handling of hazardous chemicals, related to methamphetamine labs.

  A. *(Objective)* – To hold four training sessions dealing with recognition, identification and handling of hazardous chemicals as it relates to methamphetamine labs. (**Performance Indicator** – Number of Law Enforcement Officers in attendance.)

    1. *(Activity)* – Publish notification inter-agency communication of quarterly training.

    2. *(Activity)* – Training to be conducted by members of the Task Force and Methamphetamine Laboratory Response Team.

3. *(Goal)* – Conduct Community education training for the identification of drugs, symptoms of drug use and associated paraphernalia and chemicals.

  A *(Objective)* – To hold a minimum of two community training sessions dealing with recognition, identification of illegal drugs/paraphernalia and chemicals. (**Performance Indicator** – Number of Community members in attendance.)

    1. *(Activity)* – Publish notification through local media of training date, time and location.

    2. *(Activity)* – Training to be conducted by members of Task Force and Methamphetamine Laboratory Response Team.

4. (Goal) – Reduce the illegal importation, manufacture, distribution, possession and improper use of drugs and dangerous substances including methamphetamine labs through targeted multi-jurisdictional investigations.

  A. *(Objective)* – Aggressively target top ten list of known distributors/suppliers and cooks of illegal drugs. (**Performance Indictors** – Number of cases filed during grant period, amount and type of drugs seized, number of Meth labs seized.)

    1. *(Activity)* – Identify the top ten list through regular schedule meetings with members of the Task Force and Law Enforcement agency representatives of Canadian County.

Figure 4.4. *(Continued)*

2. (*Activity*) – Development of informants and co-operating individuals through exchange of information between task force members and other Law Enforcement Agencies.

3. (*Activity*) – Increase communications between the District Attorneys Office and members of the Drug Task Force

B. (*Objective*) – Increase the safety of citizens by reducing drug related crime and violence. (***Performance Indicators***-Number of arrest by drug offenses and drug related activity)

1. (Activity) – Increase the number of buys/busts of lower level user/dealer.

2. (Activity) – Drug Offenders will be interviewed and intelligence will be reviewed so targets of top ten list can be identified.

APPLICATION NARRATIVE
EVALUATION PLAN

- To determine a project's effectiveness, an Evaluation Plan must be established. An Evaluation Plan describes the overall approach that will be used to determine the project's success, or lack of success, in meeting the goals and objectives and a mechanism to report this information. The information from the Evaluation Plan is used to assess and redirect the project, if the project does not achieve the expected results.

- An Evaluation Plan **must** include what data will be collected, how and when the data will be collected, who will collect it and when and how it will be reported and who will report it. The report must compare the actual performance that occurred with the planned goals, objectives and activities.

- Do **not** delete these instructions. If more space is necessary, use additional pages.

For the proposed grant year of 2002–2003, the evaluation of the program progress will be reviewed quarterly by means of:

1. The number of informants/co-operating individuals developed
2. The number of cases initiated from top ten list
3. Number of arrests made by category
4. The number of Clan Labs investigated
5. Amount of Narcotics seized
6. Number of Law Enforcement Officers receiving training in recognition, identification and handling of hazardous chemicals as it relates to methamphetamine labs
7. Number of Community Members receiving training dealing with recognition of illegal drugs/paraphernalia and chemicals.

Figure 4.4. (*Continued*)

With reports being evaluated by the Project Director, members of Drug Task Force and members of Canadian County Law Enforcement agencies attending the regular scheduled meetings.

Additionally;

The Program will further be evaluated for the proposed increase of Certified Clan Lab Officers working with the Methamphetamine Laboratory Response Team and the availability of the required training and on-call status.

APPLICATION NARRATIVE
CONTINUING PROJECTS ONLY – PROGRESS SUMMARY

- To assess the progress of a project requesting continuing funding, list the data collected for the goals and objectives that were identified in Grant Year 2001.
- Do **not** delete these directions. If more space is necessary, use additional pages.

Defendants

Charges:

Possession of CDS-Street Drugs	**46**	Possession of CDS-Medication	**3**
Possession of Marijuana	**89**	Possession of Paraphernalia	**85**
Possession of Marijuana with intent	**8**	Possession of CDS with intent	**35**
Trafficking in CDS	**5**	Obtain CDS by Fraud	**0**
Larceny or Burglary of CDS	**0**	Delivery of CDS	**15**
Delivery of Crack Cocaine	**5**	Delivery of Marijuana	**8**
Distribution of Imitation CDS	**0**	Conspiracy to Distribute CDS	**0**
Cultivation of Marijuana	**0**	Manufacturing of CDS	**21**

Search Warrants   **12**
Methamphetamine Labs   **19**

Approximate weight of Seized Drugs:

Cocaine	**2.25 ounces**
Crack Cocaine	**7.2 grams**
Marijuana	**7.28 pounds**
Methamphetamine	**5 ounces**
Heroin	**2 grams**
Pseudo Pills (Manufacturing)	**936 (108 bottles)**

Figure 4.4.   (*Continued*)

The 2001–2002 project goals and objectives were met in the following manner:

1. The continuation of the multi-agency task force agreement between seven of the eight law enforcement agencies within Canadian County. The only agency not participating in the task force agreement declined to do so because of conflict within the County Law Enforcement agencies. However this agency supplied important intelligence information throughout the year as well as served as host agency of monthly intelligence meetings.

2. All current task force members received Clan Lab Certification within the project year.

3. One member attended the Okla. Bureau of Narcotic's 80 hour investigator training.

4. Public educations/awareness was achieved by distribution of literature to convenience stores and other public gathering places (Wal-Mart, grocery stories) of Clan Lab components. Individual instruction and meetings were made with convenience store managers, employees as well as Lost Prevention Personnel at Wal-Marts for early detection of individuals purchasing precursors.

OVERALL BUDGET SUMMARY

CATEGORY	FEDERAL FUNDS REQUESTED	MATCH	TOTAL PROJECT COST
A. Personnel	$ 93,726.00		
B. Personnel Benefits		$ 40,584.00	
C. Equipment			
D. Travel			
E. Supplies			
F. Operating Expense			
G. Contractor/Consultant Expense			
H. Facilites/Rental Expense			
I. Confidential Funds		$ 3,000.00	$ 3,000.00
J. Other			
TOTAL			

Figure 4.4. (*Continued*)

DETAILED BUDGET NARRATIVE
CATEGORY A and B – PERSONNEL AND PERSONNEL BENEFITS

Directions: List each position by title. Show the annual salary rate and percentage of time to be devoted to the project. Fringe benefits should be based on an established formula.

Position	#	Total Annual Salary	% of Time Devoted	Federal Funds Requested	Match	Total Project Cost
Investigator	1	$ 27,216.00	100	$ 27,216.00	$ 11,785.00	$ 39,001.00
Detective	1	$ 26,125.00	100	$ 26,125.00	$ 11,312.00	$ 37,437.00
Detective	1	$ 26,125.00	100	$ 26,125.00	$ 11,312.00	$ 37,437.00
Supervisor	1	$ 35,652.00	40	$ 14,260.00	$ 6,175.00	$ 20,435.00
TOTAL DIRECT SALARIES				**$ 93,726.00**	**$ 40,587.00**	**$ 134,310.00**
TOTAL SALARIES X .433 % **= TOTAL BENEFITS**				**$ 40,584.00**		
TOTAL PERSONNEL BUDGET				**$ 134,310.00**		

Budget Narrative:

Provide a more detailed explanation of the personnel that will be assigned to the project. The narrative should briefly describe the responsibilities of each of the positions. Use additional pages if necessary.

The Investigator is supplied by the Canadian County Sheriff's Department. Investigator Carrell is the senior member of the Task Force. The two Detectives are supplied by the El Reno Police Department. Det. Garnand has been a member of the Task Force since 2000 and Det. Webster was assigned to the Task Force in 2001. Lt. Brown is the Investigation Division Commander of the El Reno Police Department and has served as the Task Force Supervisor since 2000.

The combined three (3) Investigator/Detectives will be responsible for the active investigation of narcotic violations as well as the instruction/presentation to Law Enforcement and Community members in the awareness of narcotic violations and drug identification. Inv. Carrell, Det. Garnand and Det. Webster serve on the Methamphetamine Lab Response Team as well as Lt. Carl Weder

Figure 4.4. (*Continued*)

(member of the El Reno Police Department, who was a member of the Task Force full time from 1998–2000). Lt. Brown will be responsible for supervising the task force members, monitoring of project goals and objectives as well as responsible for the required grant reporting. Lt. Brown also serves on the Meth Lab Response Team and coordinating/scheduling Law Enforcement and Community Members training.

DETAILED BUDGET NARRATIVE
CATEGORY C – EQUIPMENT

Directions: List non-expendable items that are to be purchased. Expendable items should be in the Supplies Category.

<u>Budget Narrative:</u>

Provide an explanation of the equipment to be purchased. Explain how the equipment is necessary to the success of the project. Use additional pages if necessary.

The proposed purchase of one S.C.B.A. (Subcutaneous Breathing Apparatus) gear would allow each present member of the Methamphetamine Response Team to be equipped with the required protective gear used during the investigation of active methamphetamine labs. It would additionally bring the Team in compliance with required OSA regulations of the two in two out rule. The team currently has three complete S.C.B.A. protective suits and four air tanks.

Figure 4.4. (*Continued*)

DETAILED BUDGET NARRATIVE
CATEGORY D – TRAVEL

Directions: Travel must be project related. Specify travel expenses of project personnel by purpose such as travel to training, interjurisdictional travel etc.

Destination	Airfare Cost	Per Diem	Federal Funds Mileage	Request	Match	Total Project Cost

Budget Narrative:

Provide an explanation of the above category. Identify the personnel who will be using travel and the purpose of the travel. Explain how the travel is necessary to the success of the project. Use additional pages if necessary.

Figure 4.4. (*Continued*)

DETAILED BUDGET NARRATIVE
CATEGORY E – SUPPLIES

Directions: Generally supplies include any materials that are expended or consumed during the project period. List items by type, such as office supplies, postage. Show the basis for computation.

Batteries (9v)	300	2 @ $ 4.87	$ 580.00	$ 150.00	$ 730.00
Video Cassette (Stand)	130	10 @ $ 8.98	$ 117.00		$ 117.00
Video Cassette (8mm)	50	2 @ $ 5.22	$ 131.00		$ 131.00
Floppy disks	240	40 @ $ 10.97	$ 66.00		$ 66.00
R/RW CD	200	50 @ $ 18.52	$ 75.00		$ 75.00
CD cases	200	20 @ $ 6.47	$ 65.00		$ 65.00
MSA-GME cartridges	80	$ 17.00/pair	$ 1,360.00		$ 1,360.00
Nitrile Outer Gloves	100	$ 1.50	$ 150.00		
Nitrile Inner Gloves	200	50 @ $12.00	$ 48.00		
Dreager, Phosphine Tubs	60	10 @ $60.00	$ 360.00		
Dreager, Ammonia Tubs	80	10 @ $60.00	$ 480.00		
Dreager, Hyrochloric Tubs	60	10 @ $60.00	$ 360.00		
PH test Strips	1200	2 @ $110.00	$ 220.00		

Budget Narrative:

Provide an explanation of the supplies to be purchased. The narrative should serve as an explanation of the figures. Use additional pages if necessary.

Figure 4.4. (*Continued*)

The quantity of each category is approximate numbers based on the previous two years usage. The standard size cassette tapes are used to record from the body microphones during undercover drug purchases as well as dubbing buy recordings for the District Attorney's Office in case presentation.

The mini cassettes are used as a secondary recording during undercover drug purchases, knock/talk interviews and interviews with potential witnesses/informants.

The AA/AAA & 9v batteries are used to operate the mini cassette recorders, body microphones and wireless video camera.

The standard videocassettes are used to record video interviews with defendants and informants. The 8mm videocassettes are used during undercover drug purchases and surveillance. The R/RW CD's are used to store case records and photographs in case preparation.

The GME cartridges are used in conjunction with the MSA mask for operating inside of the lab environment and while obtaining samples of chemicals found during the clan-lab investigations.

The nitrile gloves are used as personnel protective equipment while working with suspected or confirmed methamphamine labs as well as handling other possible hazardous material and or chemicals.

The Dreager test tubs are used to measure the atmospheric conditions to determine the safe operating level inside a suspected methamphamine lab.

The ammonia tubs are used as a presumptive test when investigating suspected anhydrous ammonia containers.

DETAILED BUDGET NARRATIVE
CATEGORY F – OPERATING EXPENSES

Directions: Generally, operating cost are expenses that are required to implement the project, such as telephone, utilities, photocopying, printing and maintenance. List operating expenses individually.

Expense	Rate Per Month	Federal Funds	Match	Total Project Cost
Cell Phone Bills	$ 35.00 X3	$ 1250. 00		$ 1250.00
Pager Bills	$ 15.00 X3	$ 540.00	$ 540.00	
Equipment Repair/Maint		$ 250.00		$ 250.00
Cox Cable Comm.	$ 5.00 X 3	$ 180.00		$ 150.00
Printing/Photocopy			$ 500.00	$ 500.00

Figure 4.4. (*Continued*)

Budget Narrative:

Provide a detailed explanation of the category. The narrative should serve as an explanation of the figures. Use additional pages if necessary.

The three full time task force members are issued a pager and cell phone each. These electronic devices are necessary tools used on regular basis to communicate during undercover operations, surveillance work and as a means to locate the investigators during off duty hours to respond to emergencies.

The funds requested for equipment repair and maintenance cannot independently be rated for a specific rate per month. However during the 2001–2002-grant year approximately $300.00 was expended for repair to the body mics after incidental damage during normal operation.

The expenditure to Cox Cable Communications is for Internet service. Each investigator has Internet access with e-mail services and dial-up capabilities to the Canadian County Sheriff's Offices as well as to other databases for investigative purposes.

The printing and photocopying expense is for printing of handout material for the training of Police Officers and Citizen groups in the detection and identification of clandestine lab as well as illegal drugs and their paraphernalia.

DETAILED BUDGET NARRATIVE
CATEGORY G – CONSULTANT AND CONTRACTORS

Directions: For each consultant, enter the name, if known, the service to be provided, the hourly or daily fee or rate. Consultant fees in excess of $ 450 per day require additional justification and prior approval from the Director of Federal Programs, District Attorney's Council.

Service or Product	Fee or Rate	Federal	Match	Total Project Cost

Figure 4.4. *(Continued)*

Budget Narrative:

Provide a detailed explanation of the category. Explain how the consultant is necessary to the success of the project. The narrative should serve as an explanation of the figures. Use additional pages if necessary.

DETAILED BUDGET NARRATIVE
CATEGORY H – RENTAL OF FACILITIES

Directions: For this category, identify the facilities to be used and the annual rate for rental facilities.

Facilities	Annual Rate	Federal Funds Request	Match	Total Project Cost

Budget Narrative:

Provide a detailed explanation of the category. Explain how the rental or facilities is necessary to the success of the project. The narrative should serve as an explanation of the figures. Use additional pages if necessary.

Figure 4.4.   (*Continued*)

DETAILED BUDGET NARRATIVE
<u>CATEGORY I – CONFIDENTIAL FUNDS FOR DRUG TASK FORCES ONLY</u>

Directions: For this category, identify the total amount of confidential funds needed, the federal request and the match amounts.

Total Purchase of Evidence	Federal Funds Request	Match	Total Project Cost
		$ 3000.00	
TOTAL		$ 3000.00	

<u>Budget Narrative:</u>

Provide a detailed explanation of the category. The narrative should serve as an explanation of the figures. Use additional pages if necessary.

The money for confidential funds will come from match money. The dollar amount is an estimated amount based on the previous two years. The funds will be spent for purchase of narcotics and informant information.

Figure 4.4. (*Continued*)

DETAILED BUDGET NARRATIVE
CATEGORY J – OTHER

Directions: Specifically identify the funds being requested in this category.

		Federal	Match	Total Project Cost
Training		$ 500.00	$ 500.00	$ 1000.00
Fuel		$ 1000.00	$ 500.00	$ 1000.00
Drug Test Kits		$ 500.00		

Budget Narrative:

Provide a detailed explanation of the category. The narrative should serve as an explanation of the figures. Use additional pages if necessary.

During the course of the budget year, the three full time officers will attend the A-1 (Oklahoma Narcotic Officers Association) conference in Oklahoma City during the month of July. We also anticipate additional training will come available during the budget year that will benefit the officers in narcotic investigations.

The fuel cost was determined with a slight increase based on expenditure during the 2001–2002 contract year.

The requested funding for drug test kits was based on the amount of drug test kits used during the 2001–2002 contract year with an increase of $ 150.00 dollars for the additional purchase of methamphamine test kits.

CERTIFICATE OF APPLICATION

The signature below of the Chief Executive Officer certifies the accuracy of the information in this application and agrees to comply with all state and federal provisions of the 2002 Edward Byrne Memorial Formula Grant Program and all other applicable state and federal laws.

NAME; _____

ADDRESS: _____

TITLE: _____

SIGNATURE: _____

Figure 4.4.   (*Continued*)

SUMMARY

As a criminal justice professional, you may be called on to perform writing tasks that will be read by individuals outside the criminal justice area. It is important to keep in mind that in most cases they will need more information than people within the field. Always be professional and courteous—your communication reflects your agency to the public.

Writing Memos, Letters, and Email

Your tasks will probably include creating correspondence for use beyond your agency. Remember to always be professional and thorough.

Write memos for internal communication

Write letters for external communication

Provide background information in the introduction

Provide compelling and thorough support in the body

Use headings to separate sections

Use bulleted lists to highlight items

Summarize the content in the conclusion

Give the reader the next step in the conclusion

Use audience-appropriate language

Maintain a professional tone

Honor the chain of command

Proofread and edit carefully

Writing Short Reports

Short reports serve a variety of functions. Assume that they could be read by people outside the criminal justice field, and be professional and thorough.

Use a memo format for an in-house report and a cover letter and report format for an external report

Use the introduction, body, and conclusion format for the short report

Use headings to separate the sections of the report

Clearly identify the problem you are addressing in the introduction

Support the introduction with specific evidence

Summarize the contents of the report in the conclusion

Writing Proposals

Find proposals by searching the Internet and reading professional publications. Read the Request for Proposal (RFP) carefully and follow all directions. Research the grant and familiarize yourself with the grant criteria and review process.

Plan the grant carefully and follow the format specified in the RFP. The components will usually consist of the following:

Statement of the problem

Goals and objectives

Project strategy or design

Implementation timeline

Proposed budget

Budget narrative

Matching commitments

Program evaluation

Management structure and organizational capability

Civil rights assurance

ACTIVITIES

1. Search the Internet and find three RFPs for law enforcement.
2. Contact your local law enforcement agency and interview a person who has written grants for the agency. Ask to see sample grants.
3. Write an outline for a grant following the guidelines provided in the RFP.
4. Write a memo to your instructor asking to be excused from class.
5. Write a short report addressing a potential security risk on your campus.

5 *Writing for a Job Search*

A. WRITING COVER LETTERS
B. WRITING RESUMES
C. WRITING FOLLOW-UP LETTERS
D. SUMMARY
E. ACTIVITIES

Conducting your job search calls for specialized writing skills that can make a difference in your ability to land a job. Your cover letter and resume, as well as your application form, provide a first impression, so it is critical that these documents be professional and present you in a positive light.

What does an application package tell a potential employer about you? It can tell an employer about your ability to pay attention to details. Spelling and punctuation errors can present a negative impression of you. The documents should also be neat and legible. Remember that this is the first, and possibly last, impression a potential employer will have of you. The quality of your application package can determine whether or not you are invited for an interview.

Typically, an application package consists of an application form provided by the prospective employer, a cover letter, and a resume.

WRITING COVER LETTERS

The cover letter offers you an opportunity to sell yourself. This letter is a one-page document that allows you to highlight your strengths and offer a narrative overview of the contents of your resume. You should customize a letter for each job opening.

When you write your cover letter, you should follow a seven-part letter format incorporating an address line, date, salutation, introduction, body, conclusion, and closing.

The **address line** consists of your name and complete address, including email and telephone number, and the name, complete title, and mailing address of the employer.

The **date** should be placed between your address and the recipient's address. You should use the date that you write the letter.

The **salutation** should be addressed to the person who is responsible for the hiring. Do a little homework and call the employer to ask the name of the personnel director or department head if a contact name is not provided in the job announcement. Follow the salutation (Dear Ms. Smith) with a colon.

The **introduction** should clearly identify what position you are seeking and how you learned of it. If you have been encouraged to apply for the position by someone already known at the agency, and if you know that your contact person is well respected, use that person's name in this section. You should also state that you are writing to apply for the position and refer to your enclosed resume. You might also offer a one-sentence statement about what makes you the ideal candidate for the position.

The **body** should offer a narrative overview of any special qualifications that you have for the position. In this section you should include a brief summary of your education and any experience you have that makes you stand out as a candidate. You should also include any other distinguishing factors that make you a quality applicant;

Kayla Jones
1423 East Elm
El Reno, OK
Home Phone: (405) 555-5555
jonesk@email.com

January 15, 2004

Linda Smith
Personnel Director
Anytown Police Department
Anytown, OK 00124

Dear Ms. Smith:

I am writing in response to your advertisement in the *Anytown Daily News* for reserve officers. I feel that I am an excellent candidate for this position. Please consider this letter and the enclosed resume as my application.

I am currently employed as a Dispatcher with AllCall Private Security, and I have completed a number of law enforcement classes, including Introduction to Law Enforcement, Firearms Training, and Crime Scene Investigation. I am also planning on attending the next Academy Training to complete my CLEET certification.

I am enrolled in the Criminal Justice program at Redlands Community College in El Reno, Oklahoma, and I plan to pursue a career in law enforcement. I carry a grade point average of 3.75, and will graduate next spring.

I believe that working as a reserve officer for your department will give me valuable experience and assist me in preparing for a full-time law enforcement career.

I am available for an interview at your convenience, and I look forward to hearing from you.

Sincerely,

Kayla Jones

Figure 5.1. Sample cover letter

for example, this would be an ideal place to mention any special skills you possess or any awards you have received.

The **conclusion** should offer a brief summary of the significant points in the body of your letter and a call to action. Let the employer know when you are available for an interview and let the employer know that you are eager to hear from him or her. Remember that this is the last part of the letter the reader will see, so end on a positive note and hit the high points.

The **closing** should be simple. End with "Sincerely" and a comma, leave a space, leave room for a signature, and then type your name under the signature line.

WRITING RESUMES

The second part of your job application package is your resume. A resume is a one-page synopsis of your qualifications. It is broken down into sections that may include educational background, employment history, awards and achievements, special skills, and references. Each section calls for specific overview information.

As in all application packet materials, this document should be factual, concise, and precise. It is absolutely critical that you edit and proofread this document very carefully. Errors in your resume can stop your application process before you get in the door. Take time with this document and edit and proofread many times.

The **main heading** should be centered at the top of the page and list your name and complete contact information, including your telephone numbers and email address. Specify the nature of each telephone number, such as work, home, cellular phone, etc. Make the contact information as complete as possible.

The **education** section should be separated by the heading Education and should include the institution you attended (with city and state), the degree earned, the major, and the date of completion. If your grade point average was 3.00 or above, then include that information.

The **experience** section should be separated by the heading Employment or Employment History. This section should include a separate listing for each job you have held, beginning with your title and the employer's name and address (at least the city and state), the beginning and ending employment dates, and a brief description of the duties of the position. Parallelism is especially important in this section. For example, in the passage, "Duties included supervising swimmers, rescuing swimmers in distress, checking pool chemical levels, and maintaining pool cleanliness," notice that each item in the series begins with an –ing verb.

Kayla Jones
1423 East Elm
El Reno, OK
Home Phone: (405) 555-5555
jonesk@email.com

Education

Redlands Community College, El Reno, OK	2002–Present
Major: Criminal Justice. Tentative graduation date	May 2004
GPA: 3.75	
Marshall High School, Marshall, MO	Graduated 2002

Experience

Dispatcher, AllCall Private Security, Mustang, OK   **9/02–Present**
Duties included monitoring home and business security systems
and alerting appropriate parties for alarm response.

Lifeguard, Marshall Municipal Pool, Marshall, MO   **5/00–9/02**
Duties included supervising swimmers, rescuing swimmers in
distress, checking pool chemical levels, and maintaining pool cleanliness.

Awards and Achievements

President's Honor List, Redlands Community College	2002–2003
President's Scholarship, Redlands Community College	2002–Present
Magna Cum Laude Graduate	2002
Key Club Vice President	2002
Junior Class President	2001

Special Skills

Word Processing	Lifeguard Certification
Data Entry	CPR Certification
Switchboard	First Responder Certification

References

Sam Still, Manager	Barry Jones, Director	Bill Todd, Counselor
AllCall Private Security	Marshall Municipal Pool	Marshall High School
4250 Park Lane	125 Golf Road	P.O. Box 14
Mustang, OK	Marshall, MO 65340	Marshall, MO 65340
(405) 555-1212	(660) 555-5556	(660) 555-555

Figure 5.2.   Sample resume

The **awards and achievements** section should be separated by an appropriate heading and include any special honors or achievements you have received. Scholarships, honor organizations, club memberships, or awards of distinction should be listed here by title, affiliation, and date.

The **special skills** section, also set off by a heading, should list any special skills you have. Include any computer programs you know as well as any specialized law enforcement training you have received. List each skill separately.

The **references** section, set off by the heading References, should include the contact information for at least three individuals who are familiar with your ability to do this particular job or with your work ethic. Do not include relatives or personal friends in this section. You want to choose these individuals very carefully for their ability to comment on your work ethic, competency, and overall character. Possible references might be former supervisors or instructors.

WRITING FOLLOW-UP LETTERS

A follow-up letter, although not an essential piece of your application, can give you a real boost in the applicant pool. The follow-up letter is written after the interview. This letter thanks the employer for the interview opportunity and adds anything important that you feel that you might have left out during the interview.

Use the same address and date lines as you used in your application letter, but make the body reflect gratitude for the interview.

The **salutation** for your follow-up letter should be addressed to the person who conducted the interview.

The **body** of the letter should begin with a paragraph thanking the interviewer for the opportunity to interview for the position. The next paragraph should offer any relevant information that you may have left out during the interview, an extended response to a question that you feel you might not have addressed enough, and/or any special positive impressions that you may have made about the employer during the interview.

Remember that the interviewer has taken the time to extend to you the courtesy of an interview, so the purpose of your letter is to offer thanks for that opportunity as well as to leave a positive impression.

The **conclusion** of your follow-up letter should, again, thank the interviewer for the opportunity to talk with him or her, stress that you are still interested in the position, and reiterate that you are looking forward to hearing from the employer.

The **closing** should include "Sincerely," a space for the signature, and your typed name below the signature space.

Kayla Jones
1423 East Elm
El Reno, OK
Home Phone: (405) 555-5555
jonesk@email.com

January 15, 2004

Linda Smith
Personnel Director
Anytown Police Department
Anytown, OK 00121

Dear Ms. Smith:

Thank you for the opportunity to interview for the Reserve Officer position. Having met the members of the interview committee, I am especially excited about the possibility of joining your team.

Since my interview, I have updated my CPR and First Responder certification. I will be attending three CLEET seminars this month.

I am very interested in this position, and I am available to start work immediately. Again, thank you for the interview, and I am looking forward to hearing from you.

Sincerely,

Kayla Jones

Figure 5.3.   Sample follow-up letter

SUMMARY

Writing for a job search involves writing a cover letter, a resume, and a follow-up letter.

The cover letter:

> Uses the seven-part letter format
> States the job for which you are applying
> Offers a summary of your experience
> Includes a call to action

The resume:

> Uses headings as dividers
> Summarizes educational and employment history
> Highlights achievements
> Lists special skills
> Names references and gives their contact information

The follow-up letter:

> Uses the seven-part letter format
> Thanks the employer for the interview
> Adds information left out in the interview
> Indicates continued interest in the position
> Refreshes the employer's memory of you

All job application materials must be:

> Clear
> Concise
> Accurate
> Courteous
> Correct

ACTIVITIES

1. Search the Internet, law enforcement magazines, and newspapers for job openings in law enforcement.
2. Select one position and write a cover letter.
3. Write a resume.
4. Write a follow-up letter.

UNIT III

---•◆•---

Writing for Academia

6

The Research Paper

WHAT IS A RESEARCH PAPER?

A research paper is an extended writing project that uses secondary source information to give credibility to your ideas. A research paper differs from a report in that it is not simply a recounting of information you have gathered from different resources and paraphrased into your own words. A research paper typically calls for thorough research from a variety of resources, but the source information should serve to reinforce and support your ideas rather than be simply a compilation of the ideas of others.

In a research paper you will use a variety of supporting materials. Typically, we break these into two categories: primary and secondary research. Primary research is research that you gather first hand. Examples of primary research include personal interviews, surveys, and events that you witness. Secondary research comes from information gathered by others, such as books, journal and magazine articles, or Internet sites.

In a successful research paper, you should integrate primary and secondary research. All of your source materials, whether primary or secondary, must be documented both in the text and in the works cited or reference pages. Failure to document sources properly may result in allegations of plagiarism, which is the act of taking the words, thoughts, or ideas of another and passing them off as your own. Plagiarism is legally actionable, and can lead to a lawsuit against you, lowered grades, failure in a course, or expulsion from college, depending on the plagiarism policy of your school. In order to avoid plagiarism, make sure to properly document all of your research.

GETTING STARTED

As with all writing, prewriting is the best way to begin. In the case of a research paper, there are a number of questions that you will need to ask before you begin the project. If your instructor does not give you a clear set of criteria for the research paper assignment, you need to ask for clarification on the following questions:

What is the paper topic?

Sometimes an instructor will be very specific about what the paper topic should cover and sometimes the topic is left up to the student. If your instructor asks you to write a research paper about the legal ramifications of search and seizure, then you know that you are going to be researching policies and procedures regarding probable cause, whether a search warrant is needed, and recent Supreme Court cases addressing search and seizure. If, on the other hand, your instructor tells you to write a research paper about any topic covered in your Introduction to Criminal Justice class, then you will need to choose a topic.

How long should the paper be?

Often, instructors will give specific page or word length requirements for a research paper. If your instructor does not do this, then press for more information. You should be familiar with your instructor's expectations. Ask about page length in ranges: three to five? Five to seven? Seven to ten? Clarifying the page length expectations of a paper will help you to plan how much research you will have to do and how much time you need to allocate to the writing project.

What documentation style should you use?

Usually an instructor will specify a particular documentation style for a research paper. In the criminal justice area, this is usually American Psychological Association (APA) or American Sociological Association (ASA). Brief explanations and examples of both of these styles are offered in Chapter 9. If your instructor has no preference, then you may use APA, ASA, or Modern Language Association (MLA) style. You probably learned MLA style in your English classes. In any case, the documentation style will govern all the technical aspects of your research paper, such as formatting the cover sheet, setting margins, handling quotations, inserting parenthetical notations, using footnotes and endnotes, and formatting the works cited or reference pages. Choose a style and follow it closely.

How many references should you use?

Ask your instructor about the minimum and maximum number of references you need for this paper. Most of the time, this decision is left to you as the writer, but occasionally an instructor will give guidelines about references. If you aren't given guidelines, then you should use good judgment: a three-page research paper should not use twenty sources and a ten-page research paper should have more than three sources.

When is the paper due?

This is an important question. On the first day of class, your instructor will give you a syllabus. If a research paper is listed as a course requirement, ask about a due date and begin planning from the first day of the semester. Don't procrastinate—it cannot be written in one day. As soon as you get a topic guideline from your instructor, start looking for a topic that interests you and research continuously throughout the semester. Early planning makes all the difference on this type of writing project.

Brainstorming

The first step in brainstorming for a research paper topic is to look at the table of contents in your text to see if any particular chapter interests you. Scan through some chapters to see if any concepts are thought provoking. You might also start reading professional publications to find interesting articles.

Start out with some broad topics and then pare down to a topic narrow enough to be covered in the paper. For example, if your paper is five to seven pages and you are thinking of writing about search and seizure, you might narrow your topic to traffic stops and then to the legality of using a drug dog at routine roadblocks.

From the time that you start searching for a topic, you should keep a research notebook. Any time that you come across an item related to your topic, jot down the information and the source. Make your source information as complete as possible, including the date, the title of the source, and any other information available.

At this point, you might also start keeping a list of questions that you will need to answer about your topic. You will probably want to get an overview of the topic, including its history and evolution over time.

Browsing

Browsing for information about your topic is an important element of writing a research paper. Make use of your textbook, professional journals, newspapers, magazines, television and radio news, and the Internet when you are browsing.

Broaden your normal information-gathering methods for this project; you are going to become an expert on this topic through your research. You should also find a topic that deeply interests you, as you will be immersing yourself in the information.

As an aspiring law enforcement professional, you should develop the habit of reading publications that are related to law enforcement. Among those publications are *American Journal of Criminal Justice, Journal of Criminal Justice and Popular Culture,* and *The National Law Journal.* Additionally, there are specialized journals related to specific areas of law enforcement. You should make yourself familiar with these journals and read them regularly as part of your professional development. Although you should consider subscribing to those publications, you can also access them in libraries or online.

Another form of browsing is talking with working law enforcement professionals. A seasoned professional can provide you with insights, and they may have specific topics you hadn't thought about. Another valuable resource is a law enforcement union, such as the Fraternal Order of Police. These union organizations advocate for law enforcement and keep abreast of controversial issues related to law enforcement. Officials in these organizations can make you aware of areas of concern and can even point you towards resources that will help you with your research.

Controversial issues for law enforcement might have to do with gang recognition and prevention, school violence, DARE programs, and wiretap laws. Broaden your search as wide as possible when you are browsing for a topic.

Preliminary Research

Preliminary research will help you make sure that the information available is sufficient to support a research paper of the specified length. Too few sources suggest that your topic is too narrow, while too many suggest that your topic is too broad.

For example, a Yahoo search brought up 165,000 matches for the Fourth Amendment. This is a pretty good indication that the topic is too broad. Narrowing the search to "random traffic stops" narrowed the search results to 25,100 matches, while "drug dogs and random traffic stops" narrowed the matches to 1,200 matches. This example indicates that narrowing the topic to the use of drug dogs in random traffic stops would be a manageable topic for a research paper.

FORMULATING A RESEARCH QUESTION

A research question will offer you a specific area to research. This question will not be included in your paper, but will provide you with a focus area to research.

If you were writing about the use of drug dogs in routine traffic stops, your research question might be, "When is it appropriate to use a drug dog in a routine traffic stop?" Researching this question will lead you to the question of when it is appropriate to call in a drug dog and when it is not. This guided research will also lead you to explanations of the Fourth Amendment and the evolution of its interpretation, including a number of court cases that have set search and seizure precedent.

KEEPING A RESEARCH JOURNAL

Having posed a research question, it is now essential that you keep a research journal. In this journal you will record any information that you find during your preliminary research.

You will want to make sure to record information that you will need to locate the material later, as well as to include in the reference page. You will need to include a brief summary of the information, the author, title, and publication information (including the date) for the material. Don't worry about getting too much information at this point; you will not use it all in your research paper.

Make sure that all of your reference material does not come from the same medium. One of the biggest complaints that instructors have about research papers is that all of the references come from the Internet. Look for different information and try to have a variety of sources represented. Find books, magazine, newspaper and journal articles, personal interviews, and television programs to demonstrate the scope of your research.

You should also be careful about establishing the validity of your reference sources; this is one of the biggest problems with using Internet resources. Anyone can put up a Web site, so be sure that the author of the site has credentials that establish some expertise in your research area. The spin of a Web site hosted by NORML (National Organization for the Reform of Marijuana Laws) will be significantly different than that of the Fraternal Order of Police site when reporting on the use of drug dogs in routine traffic stops.

The idea behind using outside references to reinforce your ideas is to find credible sources and to establish the credibility of those sources within the context of your paper. Don't worry about including viewpoints that oppose your thesis— they can offer you excellent couterpoints that you can refute in your paper.

SETTING A SCHEDULE

The next step in tackling a research paper project is to set a schedule. If you don't do this, the paper can sneak up on you and become a crisis. You should have a due date for the paper, so you need to break the tasks down into manageable steps. If you follow the format outlined here, the steps are:

1. Find a topic
2. Generate a research question
3. Conduct preliminary research
4. Write a statement of purpose
5. Conduct more research
6. Generate a thesis statement
7. Focus research to usable sources
8. Transfer quotes and paraphrases to note cards
9. Make reference cards
10. Generate an outline from your note cards
11. Conduct additional research to fortify weaknesses in your outline
12. Write a rough draft
13. Revise the rough draft
14. Write the final paper
15. Generate the reference page

Sit down with a calendar and set a schedule. During your preliminary research, for example, you might set a goal of finding three sources a week or of simply setting aside one hour one day a week to look for sources. Make sure to set weekly tasks working up to the final paper, and allow yourself at least 48 hours between writing the rough draft and revising it to final draft form. This allows you to walk away from the paper and go back to it with a fresh eye.

SUMMARY

What is a Research Paper?

A research paper is a paper using primary and secondary resources to add credibility to your ideas. Sources used in a research paper are documented both in the body of the text and in the reference page.

Get Started

Use prewriting to address the following questions:

> What is the paper topic?
> How long should the paper be?
> What documentation style should be used?
> How many references should be used?
> When is the paper due?

Brainstorm and Browse

Use brainstorming techniques to find a topic for your research paper. Look at the table of contents in your book, review your notes, and read professional publications to come up with ideas. Look at magazines in the library, surf the Internet, read the newspaper. Expose yourself to many sources of information when you are browsing for a topic.

Conduct Preliminary Research

Conduct primary research to see how much information is available on your topic. Broaden or narrow your topic as needed to make it appropriate for the length paper you will be writing.

Formulate a Research Question

Write a research question to guide your research. This question is not included in your paper, but provides a focus for you.

Keep a Research Journal

Keep a journal of your research. Include notes from sources as well as complete bibliographic information so you can locate and document the source later. Use a variety of sources.

Set a Research Schedule

Set a reasonable schedule for your research paper. Allocate time every week or every day to work on the paper. Set a series of goals that will lead to a completed paper.

ACTIVITIES

1. Browse for a topic using Web sites and magazines of interest to law enforcement. Find three possible topics.
2. Choose one topic and formulate a research question.
3. Find five sources that address your topic.
4. Set up a research schedule.

7 *Researching*

A. TYPES OF RESEARCH
   1. Primary Research
   2. Secondary Research
B. MAKING REFERENCE CARDS
C. MAKING NOTE CARDS
D. SUMMARY
E. ACTIVITIES

TYPES OF RESEARCH

The research that you conduct for your paper should serve to support your assertions, so you should choose your sources carefully. Don't feel like you have to incorporate every source that you find that addresses your topic: choose only the reference material that serves a specific purpose in support of your paper. Remember that you are compiling information that will educate your audience about a particular issue and reflect your own ideas; you are not merely recounting the information that you have found. You will use two main forms of research: primary and secondary.

Primary Research

Primary research is original research that you conduct yourself without relying on outside references. This is the type of research that you will be doing on the job as an officer, so getting some experience now will be helpful.

When you conduct primary research, you can use a number of different approaches. Personal interviews, surveys, and personal experience may be material that you would want to include in a research paper.

Personal Interviews

Personal interviews are excellent resources. You will want to find someone who is an expert in the topic and interview him or her about the issue you have selected. Make sure to establish their credentials in the body of your paper so that the reader does not have questions about the validity of the source.

You will want to go into the interview with a list of questions, which means that you should do some preliminary research. During the interview, take notes. You might also want to tape the interview so that you can go back and check the accuracy of your quotations later. Don't try to write down everything your source says—you will never be able to write as quickly as your source talks and you will miss important information. Instead, make notes of particularly important information. Finally, make sure to document the interview carefully. You will need the full name of your source and the date of the interview.

Surveys

To gather information about perceptions about a controversial issue, you might consider putting together a survey. For example, if you wanted to find out how the effects of September 11 have affected the students at your college, you might put together a survey asking specific questions about how the attacks have changed how students travel and how safe they feel from future terrorist attacks.

After you have conducted your survey, you can collate your results and present them in your paper, either in narrative or table form. If you choose to use a table format for the information, make sure to refer to the data in your narrative and relate it clearly to your topic; a table should never stand alone without explanation.

Personal Observation

To further your understanding of your topic, you might want to include an opportunity for personal observation. If you are writing about patrol procedures, you might want to schedule a ride-along with an officer from your community so that you can witness procedure first hand. This will also offer you a chance to ask about specific incidents as they arise.

When you are using personal observations, make sure to clearly indicate that these are your observations. You don't need to provide a reference page entry, but you do need to establish the observations within the text of your paper.

Secondary Research

Secondary research refers to published sources that you will use in your research paper. These sources may include books, magazines, journals, newsletters, brochures, newspapers, news broadcasts, Internet sources, and other published sources.

Make sure to vary your sources, and when you are doing your initial research, make a note of what kind of material the source is. Documentation styles have different requirements for different types of sources.

Regardless of what type of source you use, you will need to note all of the publication information, including the author, title, publication date, publisher, and page numbers. For Internet sources, you will also need the complete Internet address so that the reader can call up the Web site.

Although it can be expensive, photocopying is a real help when you are researching. Photocopying will force you to focus on the material that is useful to your research paper and will allow you to go back to the source and verify the information. Make sure to make a notation of the publication information on the photocopies.

Using the Library

Like it or not, your best bet for finding reference materials related to your topic is spending time in the library.

You can search the card catalog for your topic and then locate books that are helpful; most libraries also have current and bound periodicals. To find back issues of magazines you can use the Guide to Periodical Literature and search your topic area. From there, you can go to bound or microfilm back issues of those periodicals. Libraries also have vertical files of brochures, newsletters, and newspaper clippings that might be related to your topic.

Another advantage to using the library is that libraries subscribe to online database services that can help you to get articles and article abstracts online. You may access the Internet at the library, and librarians are available to help guide your research.

The final benefit of libraries is the absence of distractions and the space to spread out your reference materials.

Accessing the Internet

The Internet, when used in moderation, is a great source of information. There are a number of search engines that you can use to search your topic, such as Yahoo, Lycos and Google. You will want to start out with a broad search and then narrow your search to refine the results.

The nice thing about using the Internet is that some of the sources are very recent; the negative side is that some are outdated, and it can be hard to confirm what is outdated. Try to pay attention to the last revision date of the Web sites. Citing outdated information in your research paper is a major mistake, especially when it comes to law enforcement issues, which are constantly challenged in the courts.

Another drawback to the Internet, as previously discussed, is that anyone can create a Web site. Make sure that the Web site creator or article author has sufficient qualifications to merit being cited as an expert in your paper. Many high school and college classes have begun posting their essays and research papers to the Internet, and college students often make the mistake of citing these sources as references. Try to stick to professional Web sites produced by law enforcement associations, government agencies, and professional publications. Always look at Internet sources with a critical eye and ask yourself if the author has adequate credentials to qualify as an expert.

A Word about Internet Plagiarism

The Internet also offers students a tempting opportunity to plagiarize material. Students can cut and paste text directly from Internet sites into their papers, or they can purchase entire research papers online.

You should remember that it is just as easy for your instructor to gain access to this material as it was for you. Also, born out of the easy plagiarism the Internet offers, anti-plagiarism subscription services are now available for instructors. These services allow an instructor to type a portion of your paper into a textbox, and the service will conduct an exhaustive Internet search to find a match.

If and when temptation strikes, you should also keep in mind that your instructor has a pretty good idea of what quality of work you are capable of producing. If a consistent "C" student suddenly turns in a publishable-quality paper, the instructor will automatically be suspicious. Remember that plagiarism is an act of fraud; committing such an act could cost you your reputation.

MAKING REFERENCE CARDS

Reference cards are invaluable tools in writing a research paper. If you keep these cards, then all of your reference page information is already formatted correctly on the card. All you have to do to create your reference page is select the cards containing the sources you have included in your paper, put them into the proper order, and then type the information on your reference page.

Use 3"x5" index cards for your reference cards. Place one source on each card, and use the correct documentation style to format the source information. For a book in ASA, APA, or MLA style, you will need to include the author's name (first name last), the title of the book, the copyright date, the city of publication, and the publisher.

While this text includes brief examples and explanations of each style (see Chapter 9), you may want to find more complete style guides online or at your library. Remember that the format must be exact: indentations, periods, commas, capitalization, and placement must follow the format exactly.

Make sure that when you select a documentation style you stick to it. Check the manual frequently and remember that each different type of source will have different citation requirements. The following three reference cards give examples of the same source formatted in APA, ASA, and MLA documentation styles. Notice that each style has its own specialized formatting method.

Reichel, Philip L. (2002). Comparative criminal justice systems: a topical approach (3rd ed). New York: Prentice-Hall.

Figure 7.1. Sample reference card (APA style)

Reichel, Philip L. 2002. Comparative Criminal Justice Systems: A Topical Approach. 3rd ed. New York, NY: Prentice-Hall.

Figure 7.2. Sample reference card (ASA style)

Reichel, Philip L. Comparative Criminal Justice Systems: A Topical Approach. 3ʳᵈ ed. New York: Prentice-Hall, 2002.

Figure 7.3. Sample reference card (MLA style)

MAKING NOTE CARDS

Keeping note cards with your quotations and paraphrases on them will help you organize your paper. Without note cards, students tend to use a string of quotations and paraphrases from one source and then move on to the next source, allowing the source material to dictate organization. When this happens, the paper turns into a recounting of what the references say rather than a true research paper.

To make note cards, use 3"x5" cards and write one quote or paraphrase per card, making sure to include your parenthetical notation (typically the author's last name and page number, or the author's last name and the year of publication, depending on which style you are using). You might also include the sentence that you will use to introduce the quote. The reason why including this introduction is helpful is that it offers you the opportunity to establish the credibility of the author in the lead-in.

Placing each quotation or paraphrase on a note card allows you to isolate information from the source as a whole. This makes it easier to sort your quotes by category, allowing you to place the information where it will be most effective in the paper. This will help you to break your paper into sections and to write the outline. It will also give you an indication of what parts of your paper need more supporting information so that you can do further research for the specific information to strengthen these weak areas.

The following sample note cards use APA, ASA, and MLA format. Notice the lead-ins and the parenthetical notations that are included.

It isn't necessary to include more reference information on the note card because you will have a separate reference card for every source. To retrieve the reference card for this source, locate Reeves as the author in your alphabetized reference cards. Make sure to include this reference card in the stack that will be included on your reference page.

As Time Magazine reports, "The new FBI, as described by Mueller, will shift its focus to 'prevention above all else.' The emphasis will move from law enforcement to intelligence and counter-terrorism, and agents will be reassigned from domestic units (where the emphasis is on drug-related and white-collar crime) to ones dealing in terror prevention" (Reeves 2002).

Figure 7.4. Sample note card (APA and ASA style)

As Time Magazine reports, "The new FBI, as described by Mueller, will shift its focus to 'prevention above all else.' The emphasis will move from law enforcement to intelligence and counter-terrorism, and agents will be reassigned from domestic units (where the emphasis is on drug-related and white-collar crime) to ones dealing in terror prevention" (Reeves 1).

Figure 7.5. Sample note card (MLA style)

SUMMARY

Checklist for Preparing to Write

- ✓ Conduct primary research
- ✓ Conduct secondary research
- ✓ Gather your reference materials using a library
- ✓ Generate reference cards
- ✓ Generate note cards

ACTIVITIES

1. Using the topic you identified in the last chapter, create a list of possible primary sources.
2. Conducting secondary research, find five sources relevant to your paper.
3. Create bibliography cards for five of your sources. Use Chapter 9 to find the correct format for your bibliographic entries.
4. Create 10 quotation note cards from your sources. Use Chapter 9 to find the correct format for your parenthetical citations.

8

Organizing and Drafting

A. MAKING AN OUTLINE
B. WRITING AN ABSTRACT
C. WRITING AN INTRODUCTION/THESIS STATEMENT
D. ADDING SUPPORTING EVIDENCE
   1. Using Headings
   2. Incorporating Illustrations and Tables
   3. Documenting Quotations
E. WRITING THE CONCLUSION
F. SUMMARY
G. ACTIVITIES

MAKING AN OUTLINE

An outline is the skeleton of your paper. You can provide a detailed outline—complete with specific quotations and paraphrases—or you can use a key point outline. Unless your instructor specifically asks for a sentence outline (an outline written in complete sentences), the choice is yours.

The more thorough your outline, the easier your paper will be to write. The outline will serve as a map for your paper, and using it will keep you on track.

The first thing you will want to include in your outline is your thesis statement. From your note cards, find anything that might be useful in your introduction to help establish your topic. You will then want to break your note cards up into logical categories that will move your paper along. Typically, after your introduction, you will want to include a history of the issue and a review of the literature available on the topic. From there, you might want to discuss current areas of controversy surrounding the topic.

A paper needs to follow a logical organizational pattern. You might use chronological order (the order in which events happened) or emphatic order (from least to most or most to least important).

Sorting your note cards should make your categories fairly easy to establish. The next step is to sort your note cards within each specific category.

A good way to get started on your outline is to write a complete introduction (the first paragraph) including your thesis statement. This should be labeled with the Roman numeral I followed by the header "Introduction" and then the complete introduction text.

Your next outline entry should be labeled with the Roman numeral II and the proper heading. From there, you will subgroup into A, B, C, and so on.

WRITING AN ABSTRACT

An abstract is a one-paragraph synopsis of your paper. In it, you must summarize the important information so the reader can see the content of the paper at a glance.

The first time you write an abstract it will be labor intensive, but if you follow these steps the first time to learn how to synopsize, it will come much more easily the next time.

First, write a one-sentence summary for each paragraph in your paper, starting with the thesis statement. For the body paragraphs, using the topic sentences is a good idea, since the rest of the paragraph serves to support that topic sentence.

When you are finished with this process, you will have a series of sentences that are not connected. The next step is to combine concepts and sentences, reducing the number of sentences to about half.

When you have completed the sentence combining, do it again. Your abstract should be a one-half page paragraph that synopsizes the content of your paper. Writing an abstract is an act of self-discipline, so keep at it until you have a coherent (and very brief) paragraph.

WRITING AN INTRODUCTION/THESIS STATEMENT

Use the introduction to your research paper as an opportunity to "hook" your reader's attention. The introduction sets the tone for the entire paper, so try to add a little spark. Instructors read dull papers all the time; to find one with a compelling introduction is a rare treat. You might try the following techniques to set your introduction apart from the rest:

Ask a Rhetorical Question. A rhetorical question is a question asked for the sake of provoking thought.

Start with an Anecdote. An anecdote is a brief story told to prompt thinking or to set a tone.

Present Surprising Data. Statistics concerning people's perception of the topic can capture attention.

Use a Definition. You might use a dictionary definition to define your topic.

Once you have captured your reader's attention, you need to flesh out your introduction by offering any background information he or she might need in order to understand your topic. Remember that you are moving from general to specific, so start out broad and then narrow your content.

The last sentence of your introduction should be your thesis statement. This statement is the roadmap for your entire paper, so write it carefully. For more information about writing thesis statements, see Chapter 2.

ADDING SUPPORTING EVIDENCE

Once you have written your introduction, complete with your thesis statement, it is time to take the information from your outline and flesh it out in a paper. If you have written a thorough outline, this should be the easy part.

The key to a well-developed paper is plenty of specific supporting evidence. Don't just throw an idea out there and leave it hanging—support it! A well-developed paragraph should be approximately one-half a typed page.

Remember that every paragraph needs a topic sentence, usually the first sentence in the paragraph, and that the paragraph should only cover material related to the topic sentence.

When you are ready to shift to another idea or area, begin a new paragraph with a new topic sentence. Your paper should contain lots of evidence, statistics, examples, and definitions. Remember that you should be an expert in your topic by now, having devoted so much time and effort to researching it. Make sure that your paper reflects your thorough understanding of the topic.

Transition from one paragraph to another smoothly, and introduce your quotes so that they flow with the paper. Try not to jump from one idea to another or to slap quotations in without adequate explanation or introduction. Remember that the purpose of using a quotation or paraphrase is to lend expert, statistical, or anecdotal evidence to back up your ideas and theories, so incorporate the information to clearly show how it supports you. Don't let your research materials write your paper—they are there to help you, not to govern you. You must also be sure to attribute your source every time you quote or paraphrase. This is absolutely critical.

Using Headings

Headings can help break up the gray of a research paper and direct the reader to different sections. Throughout this book headings are used to divide information into sections.

Headings are typically broken into levels. Major headings are larger than subheadings, so you will start with a large heading and then move to smaller headings for subcategories.

Headings of the same level should be grammatically parallel, and if you have an A heading, you must have a B. In other words, don't just put one heading in—you need to have at least two headings of the same level.

LEVEL 1 HEADING WILL FOLLOW ROMAN NUMERAL I OF YOUR OUTLINE

Level 2 Heading will follow A, B, C of your outline

Level 3 Heading will follow 1, 2, 3 of your outline

Level 4 Heading will follow a, b, c of your outline

Figure 8.1.   Sample heading levels

Base the number of heading levels on how detailed your outline is. Using the headings will help keep the reader interested and break up the sections.

Incorporating Illustrations and Tables

If you have a lot of statistical data, you might want to place it into a table for quick reference. Make sure to discuss the contents of the table in the body of your paper, though. The information in the table needs to be introduced and discussed in your paper just like a quotation or paraphrase.

Tables, charts, and graphs help to break up the text and are useful in helping the reader visualize the information. Charts and graphs allow the reader to quickly compare data.

When you incorporate graphics, make sure to assign them a figure number and title, and to place them as closely as possible to where they are discussed in the text. Don't make your reader search for information that is supposed to make accessing the information easier.

If you take a graphic from another source, you must provide attribution in a text label at the bottom of the graphic.

Don't overuse graphics and remember that you must discuss how the information presented in the graphic relates to you paper by referring to it and discussing it in the body of your paper.

Documenting Quotations

It is essential that you document all of your quotations and paraphrases in the text of your paper by using a parenthetical notation directly after the quote or paraphrase. Depending on what documentation style you use, this will include the author and the year, the author and the page number, or the title and the year or page number if there is no author listed.

For the technical aspects of introducing quotations and formatting parenthetical notations, refer to Chapter 9 on documentation style.

Remember that any time you borrow someone else's words or ideas, you must give the original author credit both in a parenthetical notation and in an entry on the reference page. To fail to do so is plagiarism, whether intentional or unintentional. Be careful to document these sources.

WRITING THE CONCLUSION

Now that you have written the body of your paper, you are ready to write the conclusion. This is the last thing your reader will see, and this is the impression the reader will take away. Try to end the paper with a punch.

The conclusion should offer a brief summary of the information you have presented and suggest a call to action or give the reader something to consider. In order to tie up the package, so to speak, you might revisit the rhetorical "hook" you used in your introduction. For example, if you started with a rhetorical question, you might restate the question and then offer an answer that takes the evidence you have offered into consideration.

In any case, review your introduction and try to tie it to the conclusion. This will give your paper a tidy ending.

SUMMARY

Checklist for Organizing and Drafting

- ✓ Make an outline
- ✓ Write an abstract
- ✓ Write an introduction
- ✓ Write a thesis statement
- ✓ Add supporting evidence
- ✓ Include headings
- ✓ Document quotations
- ✓ Write the conclusion

ACTIVITIES

1. Using the quotation note cards from the previous chapter, create an outline for your research paper.
2. Write a thesis statement for your research paper.
3. Write an introduction for your research paper.
4. Write a rough draft of your research paper.

9 *Documentation Style*

A. WHAT IS DOCUMENTATION STYLE?

B. MLA STYLE
   1. Manuscript Format
   2. Quoting and Paraphrasing
   3. Parenthetical Citations
   4. Works Cited Page Entries

C. APA STYLE
   1. Manuscript Format
   2. The Title Page
   3. Quoting and Paraphrasing
   4. Parenthetical Citations
   5. Reference Page Entries

D. ASA STYLE
   1. Manuscript Format
   2. The Title Page
   3. Quoting and Paraphrasing
   4. Parenthetical Citations
   5. Reference Page Entries

WHAT IS DOCUMENTATION STYLE?

Documentation style refers to the way you give credit to the sources you use for your research paper. If you get information from someplace else—and that includes words, graphics, and tables as well as ideas—you must give credit to the source of the information. Source information is given in two forms: parenthetical notation and citations in a works cited list or reference page.

The information and format used in parenthetical notations and citations are arranged according to the documentation style you are using. It is critical that you follow the format provided in your style. Every capitalization, comma, underline, colon, and period must be correct. It might seem picky, but the format is very precise and failing to follow it may result in a grade penalty.

The purpose of parenthetical notations is to give the reader an idea of the source so that he or she can evaluate its credibility, and to provide the beginning of the works cited entry so the reader can find the complete bibliographic information easily.

MLA STYLE

MLA style is the official style of the Modern Language Association. This style is usually used in English and other humanities classes. MLA uses parenthetical citation inside of the text, directly after the borrowed information, to give credit to the original source. Each source also receives an entry in the list of works cited.

Manuscript Format

Research papers should be typed on plain, white $8\frac{1}{2}$" x 11" paper. Use an easily readable font and size (Times New Roman, 12 point is a good standard), and double space the entire paper.

The margins should be 1" all the way around, with the running head (last name and page number) $\frac{1}{2}$" from the top, right margin. Indent the first word of a paragraph with a $\frac{1}{2}$" (5 space) tab from the left margin, and indent block quotes 1" (10 spaces) from the left margin.

You do not need to include a title page unless your instructor requests one. Instead, in the upper left-hand corner of the first page, type your name, your instructor's name, the course number, and the date.

Quoting and Paraphrasing

A quotation is taken word for word from the information source. You must use quotation marks at the beginning and end of a quotation. You must quote the source exactly as it appears in the source you are quoting; do not make changes to spelling, internal punctuation, or capitalization. Quotations should be used sparingly—the purpose of a research paper is to show your knowledge or opinion, not to show how well you can quote others. Use quotations to support your assertions rather than to carry the entire paper.

Introducing Quotations

There are a number of ways to introduce a quotation or paraphrase into your paper. One way is to name the author or source in the sentence:

> According to Louis Giannetti, "Open and closed forms are most effective in movies where these techniques are appropriate to the subject matter" (86).

In this case, since the author is named in the text, the parenthetical notation only needs to include the page number. If, on the other hand, the author is *not* named in the text, the author and page number need to be included in the parenthetical notation:

> "Open and closed forms are most effective in movies where these techniques are appropriate to the subject matter" (Giannetti 86).

Notice that there is no punctuation between the author and page, and that the period goes after the notation.

Formatting Quotations

If a quotation as it appears in your paper is four or fewer lines, incorporate it into the text using quotation marks.

> According to John Vivian, author of <u>The Media of Mass Communication</u>, "Record companies claim that home dubbing has eroded 20 percent of their sales—$1.5 billion a year worldwide" (120).

> Pirating poses a serious threat to the recording industry. "Record companies claim that home dubbing has eroded 20 percent of their sales—$1.5 billion a year worldwide" (Vivian 120).

If a quotation is more than four lines, introduce it with a colon, begin a new line for the quotation, double space the entire quotation, indent all of the lines 1" from the left margin, and do not use quotation marks. Place the ending punctuation at the end of the quotation and place the parenthetical notation after the ending punctuation.

> According to John Vivian, author of <u>The Media of Mass Communication</u>:

> Criminal Piracy involves dubbing records and videos and selling the dubs. An estimated 20 to 30 percent of the records and tapes sold are from shadowy pirate sources, mostly in Asia but also in other countries, including Saudi Arabia. These pirate operations have no A&R, royalty or promotion expenses. They dub CDs and tapes produced by legitimate companies and sell them through black-market channels. Their costs are low, their profits are high. (122)

Music pirating has had a profound effect on the United States recording industry:

> Criminal Piracy involves dubbing records and videos and selling the dubs. An estimated 20 to 30 percent of the records and tapes sold are from shadowy pirate sources, mostly in Asia but also in other countries, including Saudi Arabia. These pirate operations have no A&R, royalty or promotion expenses. They dub CDs and tapes produced by legitimate companies and sell them through black-market channels. Their costs are low, their profits are high. (Vivian 122)

Altered Quotations

Occasionally, you might want to use only a small part of a quotation, so you need to indicate that you have omitted something by using ellipses. If you are only using a few select words from a quotation and the omission does not lend itself to misinterpretation, then you don't need to use ellipses, but if the omission might result in a change in meaning or potential misunderstanding, you should use an ellipsis to show where the material has been omitted. An ellipsis is three periods separated by spaces (. . .).

> "Criminal Piracy involves dubbing records and videos and selling the dubs . . . from shadowy pirate sources, mostly in Asia . . ." (Vivian 122).

If a word is misspelled in a quotation, follow the misspelled word with (sic) to show that the error is not yours.

> "The Prezident [sic] was on hand for the parade." (Person 105)

If you need to insert information to make a reference clear, place the added information in brackets.

> "Jackie and Jill brought her [Jackie's] car."

Finally, if you are using a quote within a quote, use double quotation marks to set off the beginning and end of the entire quote, and use single quotation marks to set off the internal quote.

> "Some songs repeat their simple and explicitly sexual messages over and over, as many as 15 to 30 times in one song. Said a spokesperson from the Parents Music Resource Center, 'I can't believe it's not getting through. It's getting into the subconscious even if they can't recite the lyrics.' " (Vivian 123)

The works cited entry for this source is:

> Vivian, John. The Media of Mass Communication. 6th ed. Boston: Pearson, 2003.

Parenthetical Citations

Parenthetical notation refers the reader directly to the entry on the works cited page. To find the entry for

> "Open and closed forms are most effective in movies where these techniques are appropriate to the subject matter" (Giannetti 86).

the reader would simply turn to the works cited page, look in alphabetical order for the author's name, and go straight to the entry. The Giannetti entry would appear as:

> Giannetti, Louis. <u>Understanding Movies</u>. 8th ed. Upper Saddle River: Prentice Hall, 1999.

If you are citing a work with no named author, you may use the name of the article in full or shortened form and the page number for the parenthetical citation. Just make sure that the notation clearly guides the reader to the works cited page entry. For example:

> "The command center also receives DirecTV service, which means officers on the scene of a critical incident can observe the information being released by television news channels" ("Florida Sheriff's Office Uses Broadband" 18).

refers back to:

> "Florida Sheriff's Office Uses Broadband Satellite Service." <u>The Police Chief</u> July 2003:18.

In some cases, such as unpaginated Web sites and single page sources, you will provide only the author's name or the title. For example, the parenthetical citation for the following entry would be (The Infinite Mind).

> <u>The Infinite Mind: The Bipolar Child</u>. Licthstein Creative Media. 20 Sept. 2000. 30 Apr. 2002. <http://www.ifigetoutalive.com/mind133.htm>.

Works Cited Page Entries

The works cited page should begin on a new page and should be numbered continuously with the rest of the paper. The entire works cited page should be double spaced with 1" margins and the running head $\frac{1}{2}$" from the top of the paper in the upper right-hand corner.

Title the page Works Cited and center the title. The entries on the works cited page should be listed in alphabetical order, and the first line of each entry should be on the 1" margin with all subsequent lines indented an additional $\frac{1}{2}$".

Books

General Rules

Author's Name Begin with the author's name in reverse order with a comma separating the first and last name and a period after the name section. Omit titles and degrees such as Dr., PhD, or MD.

> Vivian, John.

Book Title Follow the author's name with the title of the book. Use the title exactly as it appears on the title page. If there is a subtitle, separate it from the main title with a colon. Underline the title of the book and follow the title with a period unless the title ends with other punctuation; in this case, use the punctuation in the title. If there is an edition number listed, place it after the period and use another period after the edition information.

> The Media of Mass Communication. 6th ed.

Publication Information Look at the title page and the copyright page to find the publication information. Use the first city listed on the title page followed by a colon and the publisher's name. Place a comma after the publisher's name and then follow it with the publication year (use the most recent year listed if more than one year is given) and end the entry with a period.

> Boston: Pearson, 2003.

Book with One Author

> Giannetti, Louis. Understanding Movies. 8th ed. Upper Saddle River: Prentice Hall, 1999.
>
> Harris, Joanne. Coastliners: a Novel. New York: Morrow, 2002.

Two or More Books by the Same Author

If you have two or more books by the same author, list the author only in the first entry, and then in subsequent entries use three dashes in place of the author's name (---). Alphabetize the books by title.

> Morrison, Toni. Jazz. New York: Plume-Penguin, 1992.
>
> ---. Sula. New York: Plume-Penguin, 1992.
>
> ---. The Bluest Eye. New York: Plume-Penguin, 1994.

Book by Two or More Authors

For a book by two or more authors, use the author's names presented in the order on the title page. Reverse the first and last names of only the first author, add a comma, and then list the other authors first name first.

> Tabachnick, Barbara G., and Linda S. Fidell. Using Multivariate Statistics. 2nd ed. New York: HarperCollins, 1989.

If there are more than three authors, use only the first author's name, comma, and et al (and others), followed by a period.

> Smith, Jean Q., et al. Still Using Multivariate Statistics. 3rd ed. New York: Harper-Collins, 2004.

Book by a Corporate Author

> National Council of Teachers of English. Technical and Business Communica-tion: Bibliographic Essays for Teachers and Corporate Trainers. Ed. Charles H. Sides. Urbana: NCTE, 1989.

Pamphlet

> Oklahoma Police Corps: Leadership Excellence. Oklahoma City: Oklahoma
> Dept. of Public Safety, 2001.

Government Publication

> United States Department of Education. Getting Ready for College: A Handbook
> for Parents of Students in the Middle and Junior High. Washington D.C.:
> Dept. of Education, 1997.

Periodicals

General Rules

Author's Name Begin with the author's name just as you did with a book.

Article Title Use the title as it appears on the article, but enclose it in quotation marks
and do not underline it. Place a period after the title (but inside the quotation marks).

Publication Information Place the name of the periodical after the title and underline the periodical title. Next, provide the volume number, publication date, a
colon, and the page numbers.

> Tough, Paul. "The Alchemy of OxyContin." The New York Times Magazine 29
> July 2003: 32–37.

Newspaper Article

Provide the title of the newspaper, omitting "The." For a national newspaper, do
not include the city of publication, but for a local paper include the town in brackets
after the title.

> Hammert, Pat. "Council Makes Final Decision on City Manager." El Reno Tri-
> bune [El Reno, OK] 9 Mar. 2003: 1A+.

Magazine Article

> Tough, Paul. "The Alchemy of OxyContin." The New York Times Magazine 29
> July 2003: 32–37.

Anonymous Article

> "Florida Sheriff's Office Uses Broadband Satellite Service." The Police Chief
> July 2003: 18

Non-Print Sources

Television or Radio Program

> "Perfect Circles." Six Feet Under. HBO2. 13 Sept. 2003.

Sound Recording

> Kilcher, Jewel. <u>A Night Without Armor</u>. Harper Audio-HarperCollins, 1998.

> Parton, Dolly. <u>Heartsongs</u>. Columbia, 1994.

Film or Video Recording

> <u>The Ring</u>. Dir. Gore Vibrinski. Perf. Naomi Watts, Martin Henderson, and Brian Cox. Dreamworks, 2002.

Personal Interview

> Rupp, Alexandra. Personal Interview. 2 Aug. 2003.

> Smith, Joe. Telephone Interview. 10 July 2003.

> Rogers, Jerry. Email Interview. 15 Aug. 2003.

Electronic Publications

General Rules

Internet sources vary in the information provided by the Web site, so making these entries will require some adaptation. In general, follow the same format as you would with any other source; start with the author, last name first ending with a period; follow this with the title of the Web page, placed in quotation marks and ending with a period; next, add information about the publication; and finally, include the date of the publication or latest update followed by a period, the date that you accessed the Web site, and the complete Web site address set off in angle brackets (< >). End the citation with a period. If all of the information is not available, cite what you can find and put it into the appropriate format.

Internet Site

> <u>Redlands Community College</u>. 2003. 10 Aug. 2003 <www.redlandscc.edu>.

Article in an Online Periodical

> Bennett, Brian. "The Hussein Brothers are Laid to Rest." <u>Time Online</u> Edition 2 Aug. 2003. 2 Aug. 2003 <http://www.time.com/time/world/article/0,8599,472784,00.html>.

> Bogdanich, Walt. "Criminals Focus on Weak Link in Banking: A.T.M. Network." <u>New York Times Online</u>. 2 Aug. 2003. 10 Aug. 2003 <http://www.nytimes.com/2003/08/03/national/03ATM.html>.

Anonymous Online Article

> "Voluntary Rationing Helping Ease Water Worries." <u>El Reno Tribune</u>. 2 Aug. 2003 <http://www.elrenotribune.com>.

Marie 1

Trinia Marie

Mrs. Rupp

English Comp I

May 5, 2002

The Wiggly One's:

How Often Are They Being Properly Diagnosed?

He stood upon the grassy hill patiently waiting for—no wait—that is incorrect. He could not because he couldn't stand still. He was suffering from ADHD (Attention Deficit Hyperactivity Disorder), or was he? It seems today that many children with specific symptoms are diagnosed with ADHD or ADD (Attention Deficit Disorder) and subsequently placed on medication, but many of these individuals may be over diagnosed. An estimated three to five percent of school-age children suffer from ADHD. Many of these children are been given some type of medication. Even preschoolers are not immune to this. In fact, some findings revealed that the number of preschoolers on methylphenidate (the generic form of Ritalin) has increased two to three times from 1991 to 1995, in children ages two to four (Vatz). This is just one result of over diagnosis.

Unfortunately, far too often in today's society mental disorders are almost like an epidemic. ADHD appears to be one of them, but why is ADHD over diagnosed? Most likely it is partially the result of improper diagnosis. In fact, when comparing ADHD with other disorders, ADHD has been known to have some very similar characteristics of other disorders and conditions.

Bipolar disorder is just one of many examples of these conditions. Tantrums, mood swings, irritability: these are seen as symptoms of ADHD but are also the result of bipolar disorder. As Dr. Papolos, psychiatrist and associate professor of psychiatry at Albert Einstein College of Medicine, explains it, "early-onset bipolar is often characterized in infancy by difficulty in settling the child

Figure 9.1. Sample MLA research paper. Reprinted by permission of Trinia Marie.

Marie 2

for sleep, and sleep disruptions. By the time the child is in school, parents and teachers often start

to notice hyperactivity, fidgetiness, and difficulty in paying attention... (Licthstein Creative

Media)

Sound familiar? These symptoms sound a lot like ADHD symptoms. In fact, 94 percent of

bipolar children display some of the same characteristics as an ADHD child. But, in this instance,

misdiagnosis can have dire results for the unfortunate child. As Popolos's noted of the children

being administered stimulants alone, many required hospitalization from increased mania, violent

behaviors, and psychosis. And of those being administered antidepressants, reactions were even

worse (Licthstein Creative Media).

But bipolar disorder isn't the only problem that can appear to be ADHD. Some physical

problems, such as high levels of sugar, may mimic ADHD and result in over diagnosis. The effects

produced by too much sugar may make one think a child is suffering from ADHD. Additionally,

vision or hearing difficulties are sometimes thought to be ADHD. Perhaps a child is disobedient

and always ignoring the teacher. When others are sitting quietly this child is gazing around the

room seemingly unable to stay focused for very long. But this child's problem isn't an attention

problem; this child is having a difficult time understanding the teacher because of a hearing

impairment. Torrette's syndrome is another disorder that may mimic ADHD. Suppose a child hits

or kicks the other children. He frequently displays impulsive behavior and has difficulty learning.

Does this child have ADHD or Torrette's syndrome? Both disorders may result in problems with

aggression, impulsiveness, and destructive behaviors, and both disorders may result in problems in

school (Berkow et al 312-313). Or, perhaps, instead a sufferer has a completely different problem,

like a learning disability and has symptoms of inattentiveness or has had a recent trauma and now

is displaying undesirable behaviors. There are many possibilities that may result in misdiagnosis...

Figure 9.1. *(Continued)*

Marie 3

Works Cited

Berkow, Robert, Mark H. Beers, Robert M. Bogin, Andrew J. Fletcher, eds. Merck Manual of

    Medical Information. Home ed. New York: Pocket Books-Simon & Schuster, 1997.

Mehl-Mandrona, Lewis. "Attention Deficit/ Hyperactivity Disorder. (ADHD): Conventional,

    Innovative, and Alternative Therapies for the 21st Century." The Healing Center Online.

    30, Apr. 2002. <http://healing-arts.org/children/ADHD/>.

Licthstein Creative Media. The Infinite Mind: The Bipolar Child. 20, Sept. 2000. 30, Apr. 2002.

    <http://www.ifigetoutalive.com/mind133.htm>.

United States National Institute of Health. "Diagnosis and Treatment of Attention Deficit

    Hyperactivity Disorder." NIH Consensus Developmental Conference Statement Online.

    16-18 Nov. 1998. 1 May 2002. <http://consensus.nih.gov/cons/110/110_ statement.htm >.

Vatz, Richard E. "Problems in Diagnosing and Treating ADD/ADHD. (attention deficit disorder,

    attention deficit hyperactivity disorder)" USA Today. Mar. 2001. 5 May. 2002.

    <http://www.findarticles . com/cf_0/m1272/2670_129/72272577/ print.jhtml>.

Figure 9.1.   *(Continued)*

APA STYLE

APA style is the official style of the American Psychological Association. This style is usually used in social science classes. APA uses parenthetical citation inside of the text, directly after the borrowed information, to give credit to the original source. Each source also gets an entry on the references page.

Manuscript Format

Research papers should be typed on one side of plain, white $8 \frac{1}{2}$" x 11" paper. Use an easily readable font and size (Times New Roman, 12 point), and double space the entire paper.

The margins should be at least $1\frac{1}{4}$" all the way around, with the running head (a shortened version of the title and the page number) at least 1" from the top, right margin. Indent the first word of a paragraph $\frac{1}{2}$" (5 spaces) from the left margin and indent block quotes 1" (10 spaces) from the left margin.

The Title Page

The APA Publication Manual does not offer instructions specifically for students writing research papers. You should ask your instructor if a title page is required and follow the format your instructor requests.

Quoting and Paraphrasing

A quotation is taken word for word from the information source. You must use quotation marks at the beginning and end of a quotation. You must quote the source exactly as it appears in the source you are quoting; do not make changes to spelling, internal punctuation, or capitalization. Quotations should be used sparingly—the purpose of a research paper is to show your knowledge or opinion, not to show how well you can quote others. Use quotations to support your assertions rather than to carry the entire paper.

Introducing Quotations

There are a number of ways to introduce a quotation or paraphrase into your paper. One way is to name the author or source in the sentence:

> According to Louis Giannetti, "Open and closed forms are most effective in movies where these techniques are appropriate to the subject matter" (86).

In this case, since the author is named in the text, the parenthetical notation needs to include only the page number. If, on the other hand, the author is *not* named in the text, the author and page number need to be included in the parenthetical notation:

> "Open and closed forms are most effective in movies where these techniques are appropriate to the subject matter" (Giannetti 86).

Notice that there is no punctuation between the author and page, and that the period goes after the notation.

Formatting Quotations

If a quotation is less than 40 words, place it in the text of the paper without setting it off.

> According to John Vivian (2003) "Record companies claim that home dubbing has eroded 20% of their sales—$1.5 billion a year worldwide" (p. 120).

> Pirating poses a serious threat to the recording industry. "Record companies claim that home dubbing has eroded 20% of their sales—$1.5 billion a year worldwide" (Vivian, 2003, p. 120).

If a quotation is more than 40 words, introduce it with a colon, begin the quotation on a new line, double space the entire quotation, indent all of the lines 1 inch from the left margin, and do not use quotation marks. Place the ending punctuation at the end of the quotation and place the parenthetical notation after the ending punctuation.

> According to John Vivian (2003):
>
> > Criminal Piracy involves dubbing records and videos and selling the dubs. An estimated 20 to 30 percent of the records and tapes sold are from shadowy pirate sources, mostly in Asia but also in other countries, including Saudi Arabia. These pirate operations have no A&R, royalty or promotion expenses. They dub CDs and tapes produced by legitimate companies and sell them through black-market channels. Their costs are low, their profits are high. (p. 122)

> Music pirating has had a profound effect on the United States recording industry:
>
> > Criminal Piracy involves dubbing records and videos and selling the dubs. An estimated 20 to 30 percent of the records and tapes sold are from shadowy pirate sources, mostly in Asia but also in other countries, including Saudi Arabia. These pirate operations have no A&R, royalty or promotion expenses. They dub CDs and tapes produced by legitimate companies and sell them through black-market channels. Their costs are low, their profits are high. (Vivian, 2003, p. 122)

Altered Quotations

Occasionally, you might want to use only a small part of a quotation, so you need to indicate that you have omitted something by using ellipses. If you are only using a few select words from a quotation and the omission does not lend itself to misinterpretation, then you don't need to use ellipses, but if the omission might result in a change in meaning or potential misunderstanding, you should use an ellipsis to show where the material has been omitted. An ellipsis is three periods separated by spaces (. . .).

> "Criminal Piracy involves dubbing records and videos and selling the dubs . . . from shadowy pirate sources, mostly in Asia . . ." (Vivian, 2003. p. 122).

If a word is misspelled in a quotation, follow the misspelled word with (sic) to show that the error is not yours.

> "The Prezident [sic] was on hand for the parade." (Person 105)

If you need to insert information to make a reference clear, place the added information in brackets.

> "Jackie and Jill brought her [Jackie's] car."

Finally, if you are using a quote within a quote, use double quotation marks to set off the beginning and end of the entire quote, and use single quotation marks to set off the internal quote:

> "Some songs repeat their simple and explicitly sexual messages over and over, as many as 15 to 30 times in one song. Said a spokesperson from the Parents Music Resource Center, 'I can't believe it's not getting through. It's getting into the subconscious even if they can't recite the lyrics.' " (Vivian, 2003, p. 123).

Do not exclude reference information that is included in the quotation.
The works cited entry for this source is:

> Vivian, J., (2003). *The media of mass communication* (6th ed.). Boston: Pearson.

Parenthetical Citations

Parenthetical notation refers the reader directly to the entry on the works cited page. To find the entry for

> "Open and closed forms are most effective in movies where these techniques are appropriate to the subject matter" (Giannetti 86).

the reader would simply turn to the references page, look in alphabetical order for the author's name, and go straight to the entry. The Giannetti entry would appear as:

> Giannetti, L. (1999). *Understanding movies* (8th ed.). Upper Saddle River: Prentice Hall.

If you are citing a work with no named author, you may use the name of the article in full or shortened form and the page number for the parenthetical citation. Just make sure that the notation clearly guides the reader to the works cited page entry. For example:

> "The command center also receives DirecTV service, which means officers on the scene of a critical incident can observe the information being released by television news channels" (Florida sheriff's office uses broadband. 2003, p. 18).

refers back to:

> Florida sheriff's office uses broadband satellite service. (2003, July). *The Police Chief,* 18.

In some cases, such as unpaginated Web sites and single page sources, you will provide only the author's name and year or the title and year. For example, the parenthetical citation for the following entry would be (Licthstein Creative Media, 2000).

> Licthstein Creative Media. (2000, September 20). The infinite mind: the bipolar child. Retrieved April 30, 2002 from http://www.ifigetoutalive.com/ mind133.htm

Reference Page Entries

The reference page should begin on a new page and should be numbered continuously with the rest of the paper. The entire works cited page should be double spaced with at least 1" margins, and the running head at least 1" from the top of the paper in the upper right-hand corner.

Title the page "References" and center the title. The entries on the reference page should be listed in alphabetical order. The first line of each entry should be on the 1" margin, with all subsequent lines indented an additional $\frac{1}{2}$".

Books

General Rules

Author's Name Begin with the author's name in reverse order with a comma separating the first initial and last name. Add a period after the name section. Use only the initials, separated by periods, for the author's first and middle names. Omit titles and degrees such as Dr., PhD, or MD.

> Vivian, J.

Publication Year Follow the author's name with the year of publication in parenthesis and place a period after the parenthesis.

> Vivian, J. (2003).

If there is no publication date, use **(n.d.).** If the work is accepted for publication
and not yet published, use **(in press).**

Book Title Follow the author's name with the title of the book. Use the title exactly as it appears on the title page, capitalizing only the first word of the title. If there
is a subtitle, separate it from the main title with a colon and capitalize the first
word of the subtitle. Italicize the title of the book and follow the title with a period
unless the title ends with other punctuation; in this case, use the punctuation in the
title. If there is an edition number listed, omit the period after the title, place the
edition number in parenthesis after the title (not italicized) and place the period
after the edition information.

> *The media of mass communication* (6th ed.).

Publication Information Look at the title page and the copyright page to find the
publication information. Use the first city listed on the title page followed by a
colon and the publisher's name. If the city is well known, do not include the state.
If the city is not well known, specify the state using the two letter postal abbreviation. End the entry with a period.

> Boston: Pearson.

Book with One Author

> Giannetti, L. (1999) *Understanding movies* (8th ed.). Upper Saddle River, NJ:
> Prentice Hall.
> Harris, J. (2002) *Coastliners: A novel.* New York: Morrow.

Two or More Books by the Same Author

If you have two or more books by the same author, arrange the entries by the publication dates. If there are two publications with the same year, alphabetize them by title.

> Morrison, T. (1992). *Jazz.* New York: Plume-Penguin.
> Morrison, T. (1992). *Sula.* New York: Plume-Penguin.
> Morrison, T. (1994). *The Bluest Eye.* New York: Plume-Penguin.

Book by Two or More Authors

For a book by two or more authors, use the author's names in the order the book uses.

> Tabachnick, B. G., & Fidell, L. S. (1989). *Using multivariate statistics.* (2nd ed.).
> New York: HarperCollins.

If there are more than three authors, use only the first author's name and a comma and et al (and others) followed by a period.

> Smith, J. Q., et al. (2004). *Still using multivariate statistics.* (3rd ed.). New York: HarperCollins.

Book by a Corporate Author

> National Council of Teachers of English. (1989). *Technical and business communication: Bibliographic essays for teachers and corporate trainers* (Charles H. Sides, Ed.). Urbana, IL: Author.

Use "Author" as the name of the publisher if the author and the publisher are the same.

Pamphlet

> *Oklahoma Police Corps: Leadership Excellence.* (2001) Oklahoma City, OK: Oklahoma Dept. of Public Safety.

Government Publication

> United States Department of Education. (n.d.). *Getting Ready for College: A Handbook for Parents of Students in the Middle and Junior High.* Washington D.C.: author.

Periodicals

General Rules

Author's Name Begin with the author's name and first and middle initials, followed by periods, just as you did with a book.

Publication Date Give the date, in parenthesis, immediately after the author. Include the dates that are provided. If the only the year is provided, place the year inside of the parentheses:

> (2001).

If the month and the year are provided, place them both inside the parenthesis, listing the year first, a comma, and the month.

> (2001, April).

If the year, month, and date are provided, list the year, insert a comma, and then provide the month and the date.

> (2001, April 17).

Article Title Use the title as it appears on the article, capitalize only the first word in the title, and do not place the title in quotation marks. Place a period after the title.

Periodical Information Place the name of the periodical after the article title and italicize the periodical title. Next, provide the volume number, a comma, and the page numbers.

> Tough, P. (2003, July 19). The alchemy of OxyContin. *The New York Times Magazine* 110, 32–37.

Newspaper Article

Provide the title of the newspaper, omitting "The." For a national newspaper, do not include the city of publication, but for a local paper include the town in brackets after the title.

> Hammert, P. (2003, March 9). Council makes final decision on city manager. *El Reno Tribune*, pp. A1, A4.

Magazine Article

> Roosevelt, M. (2003, August 4) Busted. *Time, 162,* 44–46.

Anonymous Article

> Florida sheriff's office uses broadband satellite service. (2003, July). *The Police Chief,* 18.

Non-Print Sources

Television or Radio Program

> Solway, J. (Writer), & Ball, A. (Director). 2003. Perfect circles [Television series episode]. In A. Ball (Producer) *Six feet under.* New York: HBO.

Sound Recording

> Kilcher, J. (1998). *A night without armor* [CD]. New York: Harper Audio.
>
> Parton, D. (1994). *Heartsongs* [CD]. New York: Columbia.

Film or Video Recording

> Parkes, W. F., MacDonald, L., & Frank, S. (Producers), & Verbinski, G. (Director). (2002). The ring [Motion picture]. United States: Dreamworks.

Personal Interview

Do not include personal interviews in your list of references. Instead, cite them in your paper, integrated into the text as follows:

> According to A. Rupp (Personal communication, August 2, 2003) . . .

Electronic Publications

General Rules

Internet sources vary in the information provided by the Web site, so making these entries will require some adaptation. In general, follow the same format as you would with any other source. Start with the author; follow this with the title of the Web page (ending with a period); place the year (or date) in parenthesis after the author; add information about the publication; and, finally, include the date of the publication or latest update, followed by a period; and, finally, include the date that you retrieved the information from the Web site and the complete Web site address. End the citation with a period. If all of the information is not available, cite what you can find and put it into the appropriate format.

Entire Internet Site

> Redlands Community College. (2003). Retrieved August 10, 2003, from http://www.redlandscc.edu.

Article in Online Periodical

> Bennett, B. (2003, August 2). The Hussein brothers are laid to rest. Time Online Edition. Retrieved August 5, 2003, from http://www.time.com/time/world/article/0,8599,472784,00.html.
>
> Bogdanich, W. (2003, August 2). Criminals focus on weak link in banking: A.T.M. network. New York Times Online. Retrieved August 15, 2003, from http://www.nytimes.com/2003/08/03/national/03ATM.html.

Anonymous Online Article

> Voluntary rationing helping ease water worries. (2003, August 2). *El Reno Tribune.* Retrieved August 2, 2003, from http://www.elrenotribune.com.

The Wiggly Ones 2

References

Berkow, R., Beers, M.H., Bogin, R.M., & Fletcher, A.J. eds. (1997). *Merck Manual of Medical Information*. Home ed. New York: Pocket Books-Simon & Schuster.

Mehl-Mandrona, L. (n.d.) Attention deficit/ hyperactivity disorder. (ADHD): Conventional, innovative, and alternative therapies for the 21st century. The Healing Center Online. Retrieved April 30, 2002, through http://healing-arts.org/children/ADHD/.

Licthstein Creative Media. (2000, September 20). The infinite mind: The bipolar child. Retrieved April 30, 2002, through http://www.ifigetoutalive.com/mind133.htm.

United States National Institute of Health.(1998, November 16-18). Diagnosis and treatment of attention deficit hyperactivity disorder." NIH Consensus Developmental Conference Statement Online. Retrieved May 1, 2002, through http://consensus. nih.gov/cons/110/110_ statement.htm .

Vatz, R.E. (2001, March). Problems in diagno[...] disorder, attention deficit hyperactivit[...] through http://www.findarticles.com/[...]

The Wiggly Ones 1

Trinia Marie

Mrs. Rupp

English Comp I

May 5, 2002

The Wiggly One's:

How Often Are They Being Properly Diagnosed?

He stood upon the grassy hill patiently waiting for—no wait—that is incorrect. He could not because he couldn't stand still. He was suffering from ADHD (Attention Deficit Hyperactivity Disorder), or was he? It seems today that many children with specific symptoms are diagnosed with ADHD or ADD (Attention Deficit Disorder) and subsequently placed on medication, but many of these individuals may be over diagnosed. An estimated three to five percent of school-age children suffer from ADHD. Many of these children are been given some type of medication. Even preschoolers are not immune to this. In fact, some findings revealed that the number of preschoolers on methylphenidate (the generic form of Ritalin) has increased two to three times from 1991 to 1995, in children ages two to four (Vatz). This is just one result of over diagnosis.

Unfortunately, far too often in today's society mental disorders are almost like an epidemic. ADHD appears to be one of them, but why is ADHD over diagnosed? Most likely it is partially the result of improper diagnosis. In fact, when comparing ADHD with other disorders, ADHD has been known to have some very similar characteristics of other disorders and conditions.

Bipolar disorder is just one of many examples of these conditions. Tantrums, mood swings, irritability: these are seen as symptoms of ADHD but are also the result of bipolar disorder. As Dr. Papolos, psychiatrist and associate professor of psychiatry at Albert Einstein College of Medicine, explains it, "early-onset bipolar is often characterized in infancy by difficulty in settling the child

Figure 9.2. Sample APA research paper. Reprinted by permission of Trinia Marie.

ASA STYLE

ASA style is the official style of the American Sociological Association. This style is usually used in sociology classes and in criminal justice classes. ASA uses parenthetical citation inside of the text, directly after the borrowed information, to give credit to the original source. Each source also gets an entry on the references page.

Manuscript Format

Research papers should be typed on one side of plain, white 8 $\frac{1}{2}$" x 11" paper. Use an easily readable font and size (Times New Roman, 12 point), and double space the entire paper.

The margins should be at least 1 $\frac{1}{4}$" all the way around, with the running head (the title and page number) at least $\frac{1}{2}$" from the top, right margin. Indent the first word of a paragraph $\frac{1}{2}$" (5 spaces) from the left margin and indent block quotes 1" (10 spaces) from the left margin.

The Title Page

Provide a title page with the title of the paper, the author, the professor, and the name of the class. Ask your instructor for a specific format for the title page, as this varies from one instructor to another.

Begin the text of the paper on a separate page headed with the paper title in the center. If you use other headings in the paper, center them.

Quoting and Paraphrasing

A quotation is taken word for word from the information source. You must use quotation marks at the beginning and end of a quotation. You must quote the source exactly as it appears in the source you are quoting; do not make changes to spelling, internal punctuation, or capitalization. Quotations should be used sparingly—the purpose of a research paper is to show your knowledge or opinion, not to show how well you can quote others. Use quotations to support your assertions rather than to carry the entire paper.

Introducing Quotations

There are a number of ways to introduce a quotation or paraphrase into your paper. One way is to name the author or source in the sentence:

> According to Louis Giannetti (1999), "Open and closed forms are most effective in movies where these techniques are appropriate to the subject matter" (p. 86).

In this case, since the author is named in the text, the year of publication should appear immediately after the author's name, and the parenthetical notation only needs to include the page number (p. 86). If, on the other hand, the author is not named in the text, the author, year, a colon, and the page number need to be in-cluded in the parenthetical notation:

> "Open and closed forms are most effective in movies where these techniques are appropriate to the subject matter" (Giannetti 1999: 86).

Notice that there is a colon between the year and the page number, and that no ab-breviation for page is given. The period goes outside the notation.

Formatting Quotations

If a quotation as it appears in your paper is four or fewer lines, incorporate it into the text using quotation marks.

> If the author is named in the text: According to John Vivian (2003) "Record com-panies claim that home dubbing has eroded 20 percent of their sales—$1.5 billion a year worldwide" (p. 120).

Use "p." to abbreviate "page" if the author and year are not included in the citation.

> Pirating poses a serious threat to the recording industry. "Record companies claim that home dubbing has eroded 20 percent of their sales—$1.5 billion a year worldwide" (Vivian 2003: 120).

If the quotation is more than four lines, introduce it with a colon, begin a new line for the quotation, double space the entire quotation, indent all of the lines 1 inch from the left margin, and do not use quotation marks. Place the ending punctuation at the end of the quotation and place the parenthetical notation after the ending punctuation.

According to John Vivian (2003):

> Criminal Piracy involves dubbing records and videos and selling the dubs. An estimated 20 to 30 percent of the records and tapes sold are from shadowy pi-rate sources, mostly in Asia but also in other countries, including Saudi Arabia. These pirate operations have no A&R, royalty or promotion expenses. They dub CDs and tapes produced by legitimate companies and sell them through black-market channels. Their costs are low, their profits are high. (p. 122)

Music pirating has had a profound effect on the United States recording industry:

> Criminal Piracy involves dubbing records and videos and selling the dubs. An estimated 20 to 30 percent of the records and tapes sold are from shadowy pi-rate sources, mostly in Asia but also in other countries, including Saudi Arabia. These pirate operations have no A&R, royalty or promotion expenses. They dub CDs and tapes produced by legitimate companies and sell them through

black-market channels. Their costs are low, their profits are high. (Vivian
2003: 122)

Altered Quotations

Occasionally, you might want to use only a small part of a quotation, so you need
to indicate that you have omitted something by using ellipses. If you are only
using a few select words from a quotation and the omission does not lend itself to
misinterpretation, then you don't need to use ellipses, but if the omission might result in a change in meaning or potential misunderstanding, you should use an ellipsis to show where the material has been omitted. An ellipsis is three periods
separated by spaces (. . .).

"Criminal Piracy involves dubbing records and videos and selling the dubs . . .
from shadowy pirate sources, mostly in Asia . . ." (Vivian, 2003. p. 122).

If a word is misspelled in a quotation, follow the misspelled word with (sic) to
show that the error is not yours.

"The Prezident [sic] was on hand for the parade." (Person 105)

If you need to insert information to make a reference clear, place the added information in brackets.

"Jackie and Jill brought her [Jackie's] car."

Finally, if you are using a quote within a quote, use double quotation marks to set
off the beginning and end of the entire quote, and use single quotation marks to set
off the internal quote.

"Some songs repeat their simple and explicitly sexual messages over and over, as
many as 15 to 30 times in one song. Said a spokesperson from the Parents Music
Resource Center, 'I can't believe it's not getting through. It's getting into the sub-
conscious even if they can't recite the lyrics.' " (Vivian 2003: 123).

Do not exclude reference information that is included in the quotation.
The works cited entry for this source is:

Vivian, John, 2003. *The Media of Mass Communication.* (6th ed.). Boston:
Pearson.

Parenthetical Citations

Parenthetical notation refers the reader directly to the entry on the works cited
page. To find the entry for

"Open and closed forms are most effective in movies where these techniques are
appropriate to the subject matter" (Giannetti 1999: 86).

the reader would simply turn to the works cited page, look in alphabetical order for the author's name, and go straight to the entry. The Giannetti entry would appear as:

> Giannetti, Louis. 1999. *Understanding Movies* (8th ed.). Upper Saddle River, NJ: Prentice Hall

If you are citing a work with no named author, you may use the name of the article in full or shortened form and the page number for the parenthetical citation. Just make sure that the notation clearly guides the reader to the references page entry. For example:

> "The command center also receives DirecTV service, which means officers on the scene of a critical incident can observe the information being released by television news channels" ("Florida Sheriff's Office Uses Broadband" 2003: 18).

refers back to:

> "Florida Sheriff's Office Uses Broadband Satellite Service." 2003. *The Police Chief,* July: p. 18

In some cases, such as unpaginated Web sites and single page sources, you will provide only the author's name and year or the title and year. For example, the parenthetical citation for the following entry would be (Licthstein Creative Media 2000).

> Licthstein Creative Media. 2000. *The Infinite Mind: The Bipolar Child.* Retrieved April 30, 2002 (http://www.ifigetoutalive.com/mind133.htm).

Reference Page Entries

The reference page should begin on a new page and should be numbered continuously with the rest of the paper. The entire reference page should be double spaced with at least $1\frac{1}{4}$" margins and the running head at least $\frac{1}{2}$" from the top of the paper in the upper right-hand corner.

Title the page "References" and center the title. The entries on the reference page should be listed in alphabetical order, and the first line of each entry should be on the 1-inch margin with subsequent lines indented an additional $\frac{1}{2}$".

Books

General Rules

Author's Name Begin with the author's name in reverse order with a comma separating the first and last name and a period after the name section. Use the author's first name and middle initial and end this portion with a period. Omit titles and degrees such as Dr., PhD, or MD.

> Vivian, John.

Publication Year Follow the author's name with the year of publication and place a period after the year.

> Vivian, John. 2003.

If there is no publication date, use **N.d.** If the work is accepted for publication and not yet published, use **(In press)**.

Book Title Follow the author's name with the title of the book. Use the title exactly as it appears on the title page, capitalizing all the major words in the title. If there is a subtitle, separate it from the main title with a colon and capitalize the major words. Italicize the title of the book and follow the title with a period unless the title ends with other punctuation; in this case, use the punctuation in the title. If there is an edition number listed, place the edition number in parenthesis after the title and place a period after the edition information.

> *The Media of Mass Communication.* 6th ed.

Publication Information Look at the title page and the copyright page to find the publication information. Use the first city listed on the title page followed by a colon and the publisher's name. If the city is well known, do not include the state. If the city is not well known, specify the state using the two letter postal abbreviation. End the entry with a period

> Boston: Pearson.

Book with One Author

> Giannetti, Louis. 1999. *Understanding Movies.* 8th ed. Upper Saddle River, NJ: Prentice Hall.

> Harris, Joanne. 2002. *Coastliners: A Novel.* New York: Morrow.

Two or More Books by the Same Author

If you have two or more books by the same author, arrange the entries by the publication dates and use six hyphens and a period in place of the author's name in all but the first entry. If two publications have the same year, place those two in alphabetical order.

> Morrison, Toni. 1992. *Jazz.* New York: Plume-Penguin.

> ------. 1992. *Sula.* New York: Plume-Penguin.

> ------. 1994. *The Bluest Eye.* New York: Plume-Penguin.

Book by Two or More Authors

For a book by two or more authors, present the author's names in the order they appear in the book. Invert the name of only the first author.

> Tabachnick, Barbara G., and Linda S. Fidell. 1989. *Using Multivariate Statistics.* 2nd ed. New York: HarperCollins.

If there are more than three authors, name them all. ASA does not use et al.

Book by a Corporate Author

The ASA Publication Guide does not offer a format for this type of entry. For the sake of consistency, use this format.

> National Council of Teachers of English. 1989. *Technical and Business Communication: Bibliographic Essays for Teachers and Corporate Trainers.* Charles H. Sides, Ed. Urbana, IL: National Council of Teachers of English.

Pamphlet

> *Oklahoma Police Corps: Leadership Excellence.* 2001. Oklahoma City, OK: Oklahoma Dept. of Public Safety.

Government Publication

> United States Department of Education. N.d. *Getting Ready for College: A Handbook for Parents of Students in the Middle and Junior High.* Washington D.C.: United States Department of Education.

Periodicals

General Rules

Author's Name Begin with the author's last and first name followed by a period, just as you did with a book.

Publication Date Give the publication year immediately after the author. Place a period after the year.

Article Title Use the title as it appears on the article, capitalize all of the major words and place the title in quotation marks. End the title with a period.

Periodical Information Place the name of the periodical after the article title in italics, followed by a comma, the month and date, and the page numbers after the abbreviation pp. for multiple pages or p. for a single page.

> Tough, Paul. 2003. "The Alchemy of OxyContin." *The New York Times Magazine,* July 29, pp. 32–37.

Newspaper Article

Provide the title of the newspaper, omitting "The."

> Hammert, Pat. 2003. "Council Makes Final Decision on City Manager." *El Reno Tribune*, March 9, pp. A1, A4.

Magazine Article

> Roosevelt, Margot. 2003. "Busted." *Time*, August 4, pp. 44–46.

Anonymous Article

> "Florida Sheriff's Office Uses Broadband Satellite Service." 2003. *The Police Chief*, July, p. 18.

Non-Print Sources

Television or Radio Program

ASA style does not currently offer a format for this entry type. For the sake of consistency, use this form:

> Solway, Jill. (Writer), and Ball, Alan. (Director). 2003. Perfect Circles [Television series episode]. *Six Feet Under.* New York: HBO.

Sound Recording

> Kilcher, Jewel. 1998. *A Night Without Armor* [CD]. New York: Harper Audio.

> Parton, Dolly. 1994. *Heartsongs* [CD]. New York: Columbia.

Film or Video Recording

> Parkes, W. F., MacDonald, L., & Frank, S. (Producers), and Verbinski, G. (Director). 2002. *The Ring* [Motion picture]. United States: Dreamworks.

Personal Interview

> Rupp, Alexandra G. 2003. Interview by Author. Tape Recording. Minco, OK, August 3.

Electronic Publications

General Rules

Internet sources vary in the information provided by the Web site, so making these entries will require some adaptation. In general, follow the same format as you would with any other source. Start with the author; follow this with the title of the Web page (ending with a period); place the year after the author; next, add information about the publication; include the date of the publication or latest update followed by a period; and, finally, include the date that you retrieved the information from the Web site and the complete Web site address. End the citation with a period. If all of the information is not available, cite what you can find and put it into the appropriate format.

Entire Internet Site

> Redlands Community College. 2003. Retrieved August 10, 2003, (www.redland-scc.edu).

Article in an Online Periodical

> Bennett, Brian. 2003. "The Hussein Brothers Are Laid to Rest." Time Online Edition. August 2. Retrieved August 5, 2003 (http://www.time.com/time/world/article/0,8599,472784,00.html).

> Bogdanich, Walt. 2003. "Criminals Focus on Weak Link in Banking: A.T.M. Network." New York Times Online, August 2. Retrieved August 15, 2003 (http://www.nytimes.com/2003/08/03/national/03ATM.html).

Anonymous Online Article

> "Voluntary Rationing Helping Ease Water Worries." 2003. El Reno Tribune, August 2. Retrieved August 2 (http://www.elrenotribune.com).

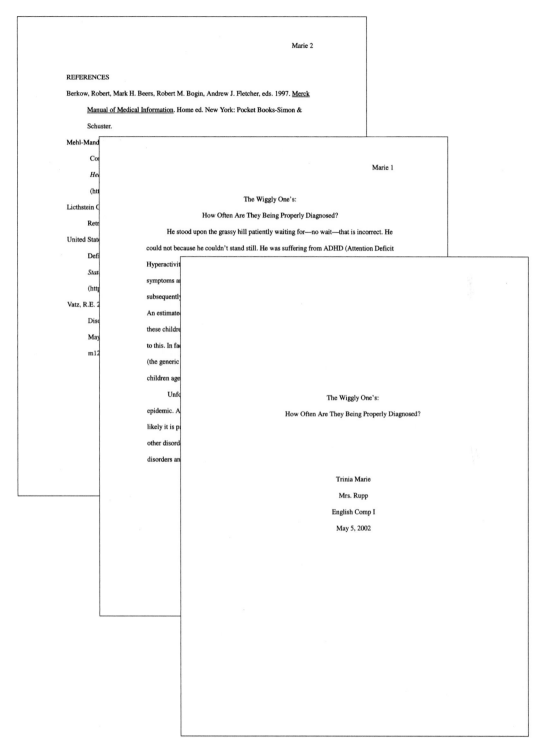

Figure 9.3. Sample ASA research paper. Reprinted by permission of Trinia Marie.

10 *A Brief Handbook of English*

—————————————————◆—————————————————

◆

I have three words of advice for writers: proofread, proofread, and proofread! Though this is by no means a complete explanation of the rules of written English, this chapter will help you to understand some of the most common errors writers make.

Most errors fall into one of three major categories:

Sentence mechanics

Grammar

Punctuation and spelling

Once you have learned how to spot the pitfalls in each category, you need to revise your writing to correct mistakes. Most word processing programs have spell-checkers and grammar-checkers built in, but many errors will slide right past those program tools. In addition, automated grammar checkers often make suggestions based on simple sentence structure, and get stumped by more complicated constructions. By learning some basic rules, you can make good editing decisions.

For starters, here are some commonly used terms and their definitions:

Phrase	A group of words	*under the tree*
Clause	A group of words containing a subject and a verb	*I sat*
Independent clause	A group of words containing a subject and verb that can stand alone as a complete thought	*I sat under the tree*
Dependent clause	A group of words containing a subject and verb that cannot stand alone as a complete thought	*While I sat under the tree*

COMMON ERRORS IN SENTENCE MECHANICS

Many problems with written communication start with basic sentence mechanics. Fragments, prepositional phrases, and comma splices and run-ons are the biggest stumbling blocks to basic competence in forming good sentences. The following sections will look at each area in some detail.

Sentence Fragments: The Dead End Streets of English

A sentence must do three things in order to be complete:

Have a subject

Have a complete verb

Express a complete thought

If a sentence is lacking a subject or complete verb, or does not express a complete thought, it is a fragment.

Subject Fragments

The subject is, very simply, the thing that the sentence is talking about. The subject can be a noun (person, place, or thing) or a pronoun. The subject can also be a gerund, which is a word ending in –*ing*. Don't let these trick you into thinking they are verbs! For example:

> Doing the right thing is important to Robert.

In this sentence, **doing** is the subject. If we take out the descriptive words, the kernel sentence becomes:

> Doing is important.

Typically, the subject of the sentence tells us who or what is doing an action, or who or what the subject is about. Subjects can be singular or plural, and yes, a sentence can have more than one subject.

In order to correct a subject fragment, you simply need to add a subject.

Missing Subject Fragment		Correct by adding a subject
Drove to the store.	(Who?)	**Joe** drove to the store.
Went out for pizza.	(Who?)	**The team** went out for pizza.

Practice

Identify the subject in the following sentences:

> Mr. Rogers and Mrs. Stone are going to the Faculty Association meeting this afternoon.
>
> The Enron incident has created a need for officers trained in investigating cybercrime.
>
> Going to the shooting range with Donna is Steve's idea of the perfect date.
>
> Although most students think that law enforcement careers are primarily made up of high-speed chases and crime-scene investigation, studies show that 80 percent of an officer's time is spent writing reports.
>
> Four inmates escaped from a prison in Texas and remained at-large throughout the ice storm.

Prepositional Phrases

Don't let prepositional phrases confuse you! The subject cannot ever be inside of a prepositional phrase. A prepositional phrase is made of a preposition and the object of the preposition, along with any other modifiers of the object of the preposition. For example:

> Over the river and through the woods, to Grandmother's house we go.

First prepositional phrase: *Over the river*. *Over* is the preposition, *river* is the object of the preposition, and *the* modifies river (the object of the preposition).

> ~~Over the river~~ and through the woods, to Grandmother's house we go.

Second prepositional phrase: *through the woods*. *Through* is the preposition, *woods* is the object of the preposition, and *the* modifies woods.

> ~~Over the river~~ and ~~through the woods~~, to Grandmother's house we go.

Third prepositional phrase: *to Grandmother's house*. *To* is the preposition, *house* is the object of the preposition, and *Grandmother's* modifies house.

> ~~Over the river~~ and ~~through the woods~~, ~~to Grandmother's house~~ we go.

Now we can eliminate "and" because we no longer have two things to be combined, thus eliminating the need for a conjunction.

> ~~Over the river and through the woods, to Grandmother's house~~ we go.

So we have broken this sentence down to the kernel: we go. It's just that simple.

> subject *(we)* + verb *(go)* = sentence

Common prepositions

about	beside(s)	like	till
above	between	near	to
across	beyond	of	toward
after	by	off	under
against	down	on	up
around	during	out	upon
at	except	outside	with
before	for	over	within
behind	in	since	without
below	inside	through	
beneath	into	throughout	

Verb Fragments

Another reason writers sometimes end up with sentence fragments is because a sentence is either missing a verb or the verb is incomplete. A verb expresses an action *(hit, run, see)*, or serves as a link between a subject and a predicate *(is, feels, seems)*. For example:

Margaret	seems	angry.
subject	linking verb	predicate

Sometimes a verb requires more than one word—they need an auxiliary, or helping, verb, such as *have, can,* or *will,* that goes with the main verb to make the verb complete. And that's where the possibility of verb fragments comes in. For example, a gerund (the *–ing* form of a verb) can never stand alone. "I going to the store," must be corrected to "**I am going** to the store."

Correcting Verb Fragments

To correct verb fragments, you need to locate the verb in a sentence and make sure that it is complete. You will often find that verb fragments are also missing complete subjects. As with subjects, sentences can have multiple verbs.

Don't confuse infinitive verb forms with complete verbs. An infinitive is the word **to** and an **unconjugated verb**.

Infinitive verb forms

to run	to lie	to give	to start
to go	to be	to have	to sit

Infinitives can never serve as the verb in a sentence.

Practice

Identify the subjects and verbs in the following sentences. Underline the subjects, circle the verbs, and cross out any prepositional phrases and infinitives.

Officer Smith found the missing child hiding in an abandoned shed.

Sitting in the parked car, the woman searched for her grocery list.

The responsibilities of a law enforcement officer are to serve and to protect the public.

A crime-scene investigation is a well-coordinated effort involving many different law enforcement specialists.

The inattentive driver tailgated the car ahead of him, slammed on his brakes too late, and rear-ended the stopped car.

Timothy McVeigh, who was convicted of the Murrah Building bombing in Oklahoma City, was taken into custody in Oklahoma by an officer who pulled him over for driving a car without license plates.

After the September 11 incident, the federal government decided to reinstate the air marshal program.

For seventy-seven hours, Jill and Allen were forced to live without television, video games, electric lights, or heat during the power outage caused by the February ice storm.

Students wishing to become law enforcement officers must have good communication skills.

Driving late into the night, Kelsey found herself fighting to stay awake.

Fragments Caused by Subordinate Words

A dependent, or subordinate, clause cannot stand alone as a complete sentence. For one reason or another, they do not express a complete thought—often because a subordinate word has made them incomplete. Writers commonly mistake subordinate clauses for complete sentences because they might have a complete subject and a complete verb and seem to express a complete thought, but, in actuality, they are missing information. For example, the sentence "It rained all day yesterday" expresses a complete thought, but when we add a subordinate word, something is left unanswered: "**Because** it rained all day yesterday." The reader is left to ask what did or did not happen because of the rain.

To spot a fragment caused by a subordinate word, look for parts of your sentence beginning with a subordinate conjunction. If the subordinate conjunction is not connected to an independent clause, you might have a sentence fragment.

Common subordinate conjunctions

after	if	that	whenever
although	once	though	where
as if	since	unless	wherever
because	so that	until	whether
before	than	when	while

Fragment: Although it might rain today.

Fragment: Because everyone was lazy and didn't want to leave the house today.

Fragment: Until I finish writing this paper.

Correcting Fragments Caused by Subordinate Words

There are two main ways to correct these kinds of fragments:

Omit the subordinate word

Combine the subordinate clause with an independent clause

Fragment:	*Although* it might rain today.
Correct:	It might rain today.
Correct:	*Although* it might rain today, I am going to wash my car.
Correct:	I am going to wash my car *although* it might rain today.

Fragment:	*Because* everyone was lazy and didn't want to leave the house today.
Correct:	Everyone was lazy and didn't want to leave the house today.
Correct:	*Because* everyone was lazy and didn't want to leave the house today, we all stayed home and watched movies.
Correct:	We all stayed home and watched movies *because* everyone was lazy and didn't want to leave the house today.

Fragment:	*Until* I am finished writing this paper.
Correct:	I am finished writing this paper. (This is not the best option because it changes the meaning of the sentence.)
Correct:	*Until* I am finished writing this paper, I can't go bowling with you.
Correct:	I can't go bowling with you *until* I am finished writing this paper.

Note: If you choose to attach the dependent clause with an independent clause, you must use a comma between the clauses if the subordinated clause comes first. If the independent clause comes first, don't use a comma.

Although it might rain today, I am going to wash my car.

I am going to wash my car **although** it might rain today.

Because everyone was lazy and didn't want to leave the house today, we all stayed home and watched movies.

We all stayed home and watched movies **because** everyone was lazy and didn't want to leave the house today.

Until I am finished writing this paper, I can't go bowling with you.

I can't go bowling with you **until** I am finished writing this paper.

Fragments Caused by Relative Pronouns

Clauses beginning with *who, which,* and *that* are another common cause of sentence fragments. Remember that these clauses usually serve to clarify another part of the sentence and can rarely stand alone.

Incorrect:	Harley is my first cousin. Who is going to the prom with my best friend.
Incorrect:	I am going to Padre Island for spring break. Which is three weeks away.

To spot a fragment caused by a relative pronoun, check your sentence for clauses beginning with *who, which,* or *that* and make sure they contain a subject and verb and express a complete thought.

Correcting Fragments Caused by Relative Pronouns

To correct this kind of fragment, place the relative pronoun clause inside of the sentence that relates to it.

Correct:	Harley, who is my first cousin, is going to the prom with my best friend.
Correct:	I am going to Padre Island for spring break, which is three weeks away.

Comma Splices and Run-Ons: Running the Stop Signs

Comma splices and run-ons are made up of two complete sentences that are run together. A comma splice uses a comma to combine two independent clauses, and a run-on uses no punctuation. Either way, they're wrong. Combining two independent clauses with a comma is like rolling a stop sign, while placing no punctuation in between the clauses is like completely running it.

Run-on:

My car broke down I had to walk to school today.

The officer signaled the driver to pull over the driver kept going.

Less than half the class passed the test the professor offered a review and a retest option.

Comma splice:

> My car broke down, I had to walk to school today.
>
> The officer signaled the driver to pull over, the driver kept going.
>
> Less than half the class passed the test, the professor offered a review and a retest option.

You must learn to recognize an independent clause and separate it from other sentences before you can correct these errors.

> [My car broke down] [I had to walk to school today]
>
> [The officer signaled the driver to pull over] [the driver kept going]
>
> [Less than half the class passed the test] [the professor offered a review and a retest option]

Correcting Comma Splices and Run-ons

There are five ways to correct these errors:

Break into two sentences
Use a comma and coordinating conjunction to combine sentences
Subordinate one independent clause
Use a semicolon
Use a semicolon and a conjunctive adverb

You will have to experiment and use your own judgment to decide which method is best for the sentence you are correcting. Always remember that you can completely change the meaning of the sentence by using combining methods.

Option 1: Break into Two Sentences

To use this correction method, you simply have to see where the two independent clauses should be separated and then break the sentences apart.

> My car broke down. I had to walk to school today.
>
> The officer signaled the driver to pull over. The driver kept going.
>
> Less than half the class passed the test. The professor offered a review and a retest option.

Option 2: Use a Comma and a Coordinating Conjunction

The coordinating conjunctions can best be remembered as the BOYFANS:

B O Y F A N S
u r e o n o o
t   t   r d   r

Remember that different coordinating conjunctions have different meanings.

But	shows contrast	*We banged on the TV, but the picture was still fuzzy.*
Or	shows a choice	*You can come with me, or you can stay at home.*
Yet	shows contrast	*I want to go with Tom, yet I wonder what they would think.*
For	shows a causal relationship	*I slept, for I was tired.*
And	in addition	*I will go to the store, and Mary will stay at home.*
Nor	neither	*Neither snow nor ice can keep me from going to the store.*
So	shows a causal effect	*The store was closed, so we could not buy our school supplies yesterday.*

Use a comma and a coordinating conjunction to combine independent clauses.

My car broke down, so I had to walk to school today.

The officer signaled the driver to pull over, but the driver kept going.

Less than half the class passed the test, so the professor offered a review and a retest option.

Option 3: Subordinate One Independent Clause

You can choose to subordinate one of the independent clauses (making it dependent) and combine it with the remaining independent clause. Remember to use a comma between the clauses only if the subordinated clause comes first.

Because my car broke down, I had to walk to school today.

I had to walk to school today because my car broke down.

Although the officer signaled the driver to pull over, the driver kept going.

The driver kept on going although the officer signaled him to pull over.

Because less than half the class passed the test, the professor offered a review and a retest option.

The professor offered a review and a retest option because less than half the class passed the test.

Option 4: Use a Semicolon

If the ideas are closely related, you can use a semicolon to combine the clauses. Use this method sparingly because it leads to choppy sentences and is tiring for the reader.

My car broke down; I had to walk to school today.

The officer signaled the driver to pull over; the driver kept going.

Less than half the class passed the test; the professor offered a review and a retest option.

Option 5: Use a Semicolon and a Conjunctive Adverb

Conjunctive adverbs show a relationship between two independent clauses. To use a conjunctive adverb to combine clauses, we need to use this formula:

Independent clause; conjunctive adverb, independent clause.

Conjunctive adverbs

therefore	however	nevertheless
consequently	moreover	otherwise
besides	furthermore	accordingly

My car broke down; consequently, I had to walk to school today.

The officer signaled the driver to pull over; however, the driver kept going.

Less than half the class passed the test; therefore, the professor offered a review and a retest option.

Practice

Correct the following comma splices and run-ons using a variety of methods.

The wind blew in great gusts it knocked down power lines all over the state.

Security for the 2002 Olympics in Utah is the tightest in history people are afraid of more terrorist attacks on the United States.

Many chain saws have been in use ever since the ice storm emergency rooms are seeing a drastic increase in severed fingers.

The officers searched the vehicle after a routine traffic stop there was a strong smell of what appeared to be an alcoholic beverage.

Racial profiling has been a controversial topic many people have changed their attitudes about profiling since the September 11 attacks.

Icy road surfaces cause many traffic accidents motorists drive too fast for the conditions.

It is sunny today the wind is very cold.

Many college students have poor study habits they must develop good habits to maintain high grades.

Television violence has increased in the past decade some experts claim that desensitization caused by exposure to violence in the media has increased the incidences of violence in society.

Insurance rates are higher for teenage boys statistics show that they are more likely to have car accidents.

COMMON ERRORS IN GRAMMAR

Don't cringe just because the word "grammar" appears in this book. There are some common mistakes in grammar that writers make, and they are easy to avoid once you learn to recognize them. Here are some of the most common grammar errors and how to correct them.

Subject–Verb Agreement

The subject of the sentence must agree with the verb; if the subject is plural, then the verb must be plural. If the subject is singular, then the verb must be singular. In order to make sure this is happening, you have to locate the subject and the verb, which we covered in the previous section. Now let's focus on making them work together.

Mary is going to the park today.

In this sentence, *Mary* is the subject, so we have to make the verb agree. *Mary is.*

Mary and Linda are going to the park today.

In this sentence the subject is plural, *Mary and Linda*, so we have to make the verb plural. An easy way to do this is to change the subject to a pronoun in your mind. *Mary* can be changed to *she*, and *Mary and Linda* can be changed to *they.*

Look at the following pronouns and the verb forms that agree with them:

To sit		To go		To drink	
Singular	Plural	Singular	Plural	Singular	Plural
I 　　　sit you	we sit you sit	I 　　　go you	we go you go	I 　　　drink you	we drink you drink
he she　　sits it	they sit	he she　　goes it	they go	he she　　drinks it	they drink

Pronoun Problems

Pronouns must agree with their antecedents, or the words they are referring to. Typically, when we speak, we say things like "Everyone is doing their best," but this presents a number agreement problem. *Everyone* is singular, so we should say, "Everyone is doing his or her best." Another way to solve this would be to say, "They are all doing their best," thus eliminating the number confusion entirely.

Indefinite pronouns are always singular. Indefinite pronouns include:

one	everybody
anyone	somebody
everyone	each
someone	either
nobody	neither
anybody	

Consider these sentences:

Incorrect:　Each of the drivers denied fault in their statements.

Correct:　Each of the drivers denied fault in his statement.

Correct:　The drivers both denied fault in their statements.

Note: Writers commonly correct pronoun number agreement errors by using the generic "he" to make a pronoun singular. You should be careful to avoid the temptation to fall into sexist language patterns, as not all drivers are male. For this reason, try to use the appropriate gender, or make the entire sentence plural, as in, "The drivers both denied fault in their statements."

Another common pronoun error is pronoun reference. Sometimes it isn't clear what a pronoun is referring to, and this is when we run into problems.

Consider these sentences:

> When he set the vase on the table it shattered.

What shattered? The table or the vase? It is impossible to tell because the pronoun reference is unclear. One way to clear up the confusion is to rewrite the sentence to read:

> The vase shattered when he set it on the table.

Another example,

> Amanda told Marie that she was jealous.

Who was jealous, Amanda or Marie? This can be rewritten more clearly as:

> "I am jealous," Amanda told Marie.

Dangling Modifiers

A dangling modifier is a descriptive word or phrase that has nothing to refer to.

Incorrect: Driving in heavy traffic, my head started to hurt.

Why would a head be driving?

Correct: While I was driving in heavy traffic, my head started to hurt.

Incorrect: Whistling down the street, my legs gave out.

Legs don't whistle.

Correct: As I was whistling down the street, my legs gave out.

The problem with dangling modifiers is that a reader cannot tell who or what is performing the action referred to in the modifier. You need to make sure that the modifier has something in the sentence to describe.

Misplaced Modifiers

Misplaced modifiers are like dangling modifiers, but there is something for the modifier to describe. In this case, the modifier is describing the wrong thing. Although these errors can be amusing, they interfere with the reader's understanding.

Incorrect: The man dived into the pool with the mustache.

Does the pool have a mustache?

Correct: The man with the mustache dived into the pool.

Incorrect: The raccoon attacked the child with sharp claws.

The child had sharp claws?

Correct: The raccoon with sharp claws attacked the child.

Place the modifier close to what it is modifying to avoid confusion.

Wordiness

Wordy phrases add length to a paper, but they generally annoy a reader. The goal in professional writing is be as concise as possible. As a rule, never write to show off your vocabulary, never say in six words what can be said in two, avoid repetition, and keep it short and simple.

Refer to Boxes 1.2 and 1.4 in Chapter 1 to review wordy expressions and their substitutes.

PUNCTUATION

Mechanical errors refer to common mistakes writers make in punctuation and spelling. While this handbook cannot begin to offer a detailed explanation of all of the rules of punctuation and spelling, this section will give a summary of the basic rules.

End Punctuation

Sentences should end with periods unless they are questions. Got it? Periods can also be used to show abbreviation, as in Dr. or Mrs. If you write a question, make sure to end it with a question mark.

Commas

There are seven major uses for the comma.

1. **Commas for introductory elements.** This comma is used to separate information that gives the reader extra information, such as when or where something happened.

    On Tuesday, Marvin will take his car for an oil change.

    After the wedding, Jerry and Lori left for their honeymoon.

2. **Commas to separate items in a series.** When there are three or more items in series, use a comma to separate each item.

> I went to the grocery store because I needed bacon, eggs, and bread.

> I want to run into the grocery store to pick up shampoo, swing by the mall to get a new sweater, and stop at the cleaners for my clothes before we go home.

Be careful to check whether you should use serial commas (commas after each item in a list). Some styles omit the comma before the last item in a list.

> I went to the grocery store because I needed bacon, eggs and bread.

3. **Commas to separate modifiers.** When two or more modifiers are modifying the same word, use a comma to separate the modifiers. Only use a comma if you could place *and* between the modifiers.

> The old, gray-haired woman drove slowly down the street.

> The tired, smelly, dirty man slept on a nearby park bench.

4. **Commas as interrupters.** Use commas to bracket off sections that add information that is not essential to the meaning of the sentence. If the section is critical to the meaning of the sentence, don't set it apart with commas. Try reading the sentence with and without the section. If the meaning is the same, use the commas.

> My Uncle John, who lives in Springfield, owns a BMW.

> Ariel, who is an accountant, runs three miles a day.

5. **Commas with coordinating conjunctions to separate independent clauses.** Use a comma and a coordinating conjunction (but, or, yet, for, and, nor, so) to combine two independent clauses. This forms a compound sentence. Make sure that the conjunction is actually coordinating two independent clauses, though; you don't want to use a comma every time you use a conjunction.

> Mary started the car, but she couldn't get it to idle.

> I was going to be twenty minutes late to class, so I just went to the Student Center and played pool.

6. **Commas to separate a dependent clause from an independent clause.** If a sentence begins with a dependent clause, place a comma after the dependent

clause. If, however, the sentence begins with an independent clause, don't use a comma to separate the two.

Because it was snowing hard, Seth decided to stay at home.

Seth decided to stay at home because it was snowing hard.

7. **Commas to separate items in an address.** Use commas to separate cities and states, as well as items in addresses.

Joe Smith lives at 1405 Elm Street, Springfield, Missouri.

Commonly Misspelled Words

—— •◆• ——

A

abrasion
absence
abutment
accept
access
accessible
accessories
accident
accidental
accidentally
accommodate
accomplice
accumulate
accurate
accusation
accusatory
accused
achievement
acknowledge
acknowledgement
acknowledgment
acquaintance
acquainted
acquired
acquitted
admissible
admission
admitted
admonish
admonition
adolescent
advice
advise
affidavit
affirmative
aggressive
aggressor
alibi
alien
alimony
allegation
allege
alleged
all right
altercation
amateur
ambulance
amphetamine
analysis
analyze
analyzed
annulment
anonymous
argument
argumentative
arraignment

assailant
athletic
athletics
attendance
attendant
attorney
attribute
automatic
automatically
autopsy

B

bail
bailiff
bandanna
barbiturate
barrel
barreled
baton
battery
bayonet
believe
belligerent
Benzedrine
beverage
boisterous
brassiere
Breathalyzer

bruise
bureau
burglary
buses

C

caliber
caliper
canceled
cancellation
capital
Capitol
carburetor
cardiac
cartilage
cartridge
casualties
casualty
catastrophe
Caucasian
caution
character
characteristics
chauffeur
chemical
Chevrolet
chief
Chrysler

circumstance
circumstantial
citable
citation
citizen
civil
cocaine
codeine
coercion
coincide
coincidence
collaborate
collar
collide
collision
colonel
combustible
commission
commit
commitment
committed
committee
communicate
communications
compensate
compensation
competent
competition
complainant
complaint
complexion
compliance
compulsory
compress
concussion
condition
confession
conscience
consciousness
consecutive
consensus
consent
consequences
consequently
consistent
conspicuous
conspiracy
contagious
convenience
conviction
convulsion
cooperate
cooperation
corners
coroner

corporal
corporation
corporative
corps
corpse
corpus delicti
corroborate
counseled
counselor
counterfeit
criminal
criminalist
criminally
cruelty
cruising
crystallized
custody
customary
cylinder

D

damage
dangerous
daughter
deadly
debris
deceased
deceive
deceived
deceptive
decomposition
defecate
defecated
defendant
defence
defense
defensive
definite
delinquency
delinquent
denied
deposition
depressant
depression
describe
description
designate
designated
desperate
despondent
detained
determine
deterrence
deterrent

device
Dexedrine
diesel
different
dilapidated
dilated
direction
disagreeable
disappear
disappearance
disappoint
disaster
disastrous
discrepancies
discrepancy
disguise
disturbance
drunken
drunkenness
dying

E

eastward
efficiency
efficient
embezzlement
enclosure
enforce
enforcement
erratic
erratically
euphoria
evasive
evidence
exceeding
exercise
exercised
exhibit
exhibition
exhibitor
exonerate
expedite
experience
explanation
explosion
expose
extinguish
extortion
extradition

F

fascinating
fatal

fatality
February
fecal
feces
federal
felony
fetal
fetus
fiber
fluorescent
forcible
forcibly
forfeit
forfeiture
forgery
fracture
fraudulent
frightened
fugitive

G

garrote
glycerin
glycerine
government
governor
gradual
gradually
gratification
grievance
guarantee
guard
guardian
guerrilla
guilty

H

habeas corpus
habitual
habitually
Halloween
hallucination
hallucinogen
harass
hazard
hazardous
hemophilia
hemorrhage
heroin
Hispanic
homicide
hydraulic
hypodermic

I

identifiable
identification
illegal
illegitimate
illicit
illiterate
immediate
immediately
immoral
immunity
impatient
impede
implicate
implied
imposter
impounded
imprisonment
inadequate
inadmissible
incarceration
incendiary
incite
incoherent
incompetent
inconsistent
incorrigible
indecent
independent
indict
indictment
information
infraction
inhabitant
inhalation
injection
injured
injury
innocence
innocent
inquire
inquiry
inscription
insufficient
insurance
intercept
interior
interrogate
interrogation
interrupted
intersect
intersection
interstate
interview
intoxicated
intoxication
invasion
investigate
investigation
involuntary
irreversible
irrigate
irritated
irritation

J

judge
judgment
jurisdiction
justice
justifiable
justification
juvenile

K

kerosene
khaki
kidnapped
kilogram
knowledge

L

laboratory
laceration
lawyer
legal
legalize
legally
legible
legislator
legislature
legitimate
lewd
liable
liabilities
liability
libel
lien
lieutenant
liquefy
liquid
liquor
litigation
loitering

M

magistrate
maintain
maintenance
malice
malicious
manageable
management
maneuver
manslaughter
manufacturer
manufacturing
marijuana
marshal
material
measurement
memorandum
mentally
mileage
minimum
minor
miscellaneous
mischief
mischievous
misconduct
misdemeanor
misspell
mobile
molested
morale
motorcycle
municipal
murdered
mustache

N

narcotic
narrative
negative
neglect
negligence
neighbor
neighborhood
neither
nephew
niece
noticeable
noticing
notification
notified
nuisance

O

objectively
obscenity
occupant
occupation
occur
occurred
occurrence
occurs
odor
offense
offensive
officer
official
omission
omitted
ordinance
oxygen

P

parallel
paraphernalia
passenger
patrolling
pedestrian
penalize
penalty
perimeter
pierce
poison
poisonous
pornographic
possess
possession
precede
preceding
predominant
preferable
preference
pregnant
prejudice
preliminary
premises
principal
principle
prisoner
probable
probably
probation
procedure
proceed
proceeded
process

profession
professional
prohibit
prohibited
prosecute
prosecution
prosecutor
prostitution
psychological
psychology
publicity
punishable
punitive
pursuit

Q

quality
quantity
quarantine
query
question
questioning
questionnaire
quiet
quinine

R

racial
radar
raid
receipt
receive
receiving
reckless
recognizance
recognize
recollect
reference
referred
refrain
refutable
registered
registrar
registration
released
relevant
repeat
repellent
repetition
repossession
representation

reputation
requirement
residence
resistance
resolution
respiration
responsibility
responsible
restaurant
restrained
resuscitation
resuscitator
revoked
revolver
rigid
rigor mortis
robbery
routine

S

schizophrenia
scissors
sedative
seize
seizure
separate
separately
separation
sergeant
severed
sewage
sexual
sheriff
signaled
signature
significant
similar
siphon
siren
skeletal
sketch
skidded
sobriety
specimen
statute
statutory
steering
stimulant
stomach
strangulation
stripped
struck

subdued
subject
subpoena
substance
sufficient
suffocation
superior
supervisor
suppress
suppression
surrender
surveillance
suspend
suspensions
suspicion
suspicious
swerve
symptom

T

tattoo
technique
tenant
territory
testimony
theft
thieves
threaten
tongue
traffic
trafficking
training
transfer
transferable
transferred
transport
trauma
trespass
trespassing
trial
tried
tries
truancy

U

unnecessary
untie
unusual
unusually
urgent
urinate

urine
utility

V

vacancy
vagrancy
valuable
vandalism
vehicle
verbal
verified
verify
vertical
victim
violation
violator
voluntary
volunteer

W

warning
warrant
weapon
witness
witnessed
witnesses
women
wounded
wreck
wrestle
wrist
writ
writing
written

X

X ray
X-ray

Y

yield
young
your
youthful

Z

zero
zigzag

Index